Demythologizing the Romance of Conquest

Recent Titles in
Contributions to the Study of World Literature

Demythologizing the Romance of Conquest

Jeanne Armstrong

Contributions to the Study of World Literature, Number 100

GREENWOOD PRESS
Westport, Connecticut • London

Library of Congress Cataloging-in-Publication Data

Armstrong, Jeanne, 1946–
    Demythologizing the romance of conquest / Jeanne Armstrong.
        p.   cm.—(Contributions to the study of world literature, ISSN 0738–9345 ; no. 100)
    Includes bibliographical references and index.
    ISBN 0–313–31067–X (alk. paper)
    1. American fiction—Women authors—History and criticism.   2. English
fiction—Women authors—History and criticism.   3. Women and literature—History—20th
century.   4. O'Faolain, Julia. No country for young men.   5. Corpi, Lucha, 1945– Delia's
song.   6. Erdrich, Louise. Tracks.   7. Brodber, Erna. Myal.   8. Imperialism in literature. 9.
Colonies in literature.   10. Sex role in literature.   11. Myth in literature.   I. Title. II. Series.
PS374.W6A76   2000
813′.54099287—dc21   99–058882

British Library Cataloguing in Publication Data is available.

Library of Congress Catalog Card Number: 99–058882
ISBN: 0–313–31067–X
ISSN: 0738–9345

First published in 2000

Greenwood Press, 88 Post Road West, Westport, CT 06881
An imprint of Greenwood Publishing Group, Inc.
www.greenwood.com

Printed in the United States of America

The paper used in this book complies with the
Permanent Paper Standard issued by the National
Information Standards Organization (Z39.48–1984).

10 9 8 7 6 5 4 3 2 1

∼ Contents ∼

1
～ Introduction ～

In women's speech, as in their writing, that element which never stops reso-
nating, which once we've been permeated by it, profoundly and impercepti-
bly touched by it, retains the power of moving us—that element is the song.

Cixous 1980: 251

Theorizing always needs a "Savage." The Savage in the West has always been
the Woman. . . . She is needed so that her difference can act as a confirmation
of man's "natural superiority" and of his "birthright" to be the best.

Feral, quoted in Braidotti 1991: 214

Women's voices and critical theory by and about women, especially
women of color and Third World women, are increasingly important issues in contemporary literary and cultural criticism.[1] The four women's
novels under consideration here concern the re-membering of fragmented
repressed stories by women whose difference has been constructed by others. Whether they have been dislocated and dispossessed of their culture
and history through the intervention of colonialism or erased through being restricted to domestic spaces where their sexuality and reproductive capacity can be controlled, colonized people and women in most societies
have often been denied the right to speak as subjects or have not been understood because their discourse fell outside the dominant linguistic and
symbolic order.

The strategic use of difference can be useful in uncovering the repressed
relations of reproduction, erased precolonial cultures and the often forgot-

ten story of colonialism's horrors—rape, conquest and slavery. In this strategic role, difference is not an argument for essentialism but for the
uncovering of sociocultural and historical differences based on race and
class oppression and the experiential differences of women's oppression.
Ramon Saldívar claims that the difference of contemporary Chicano narrative is a "difference not of kind, but of dialectical position; a difference that
allows it to retain its special relation to its Mexican and American contexts," and Anne McClintock states that women's narrative differences
speak "not of anatomical destiny and design, but of the daily difficulties
women experience in negotiating their lives past the magisterial forms of
male selfhood" (Saldívar 1990: 8; McClintock 1991: 221). Finally, Emma
Perez recommends the "strategic essentialism" conceptualized by Gayatri
Spivak as a method of "asserting countersites within dominant society"
(Perez 1998: 87).

These four women's novels can be viewed through such a lens because
their characters are situated in unique cultural and historical contexts that
determine the way the female characters, in particular, negotiate
countersites of resistance to the oppressive and repressive circumstances of
their lives. Yet these four novels all express similar themes resulting from
conflict between the dominant and submerged cultures. In these novels,
the boundaries between personal and political, colonizer and colonized,
madness and sanity are explored, and a descent into internal hells is often a
prerequisite for transformation of both the self and the social order. Julia
O'Faolain is Irish by birth and has resided in London and Los Angeles. Her
novel *No Country for Young Men* takes place in 1970s Ireland and in the period of the 1920s conflicts related to Ireland's independence from Great
Britain. Lucha Corpi is a Mexican American woman. *Delia's Song* takes
place during the late 1970s and the period of the Berkeley Chicano rights
movement of 1969. Erna Brodber is a Jamaican writer, whose novel *Myal* is
set in 1919 Jamaica at the emergence of a Jamaican labor movement. Louise
Erdrich is half Anishinaabeg (Chippewa) and her novel *Tracks* is situated
during the years 1912–1924.

Though it is important to locate each of these texts in its unique cultural
and historical context, the dominant themes of all four novels converge at
the point where their characters attempt to express a voice and identity
outside the control of patriarchal colonialism. Thus while my approach
validates the differences between these cultures, it also emphasizes the
point of intersection, that is, the psychological impact of colonialism (internal and/or external) on the characters and the decolonization process,
which requires recovering stories whose discourse opposes the hegemony.

My approach to these novels reveals the process by which some of the female characters in these novels resist the inauthentic condition imposed on them by colonialism.

Denied the right to subjectivity, internalizing and refracting the colonizer's address to its other as darkness and negation, alienated from a ravaged natal culture, the colonized is condemned to exist in an inauthentic condition. (Parry 1987: 29)

Like Ella, who develops an hysterical pregnancy and then causes a destructive storm as she is healed, the female characters in these novels are "uncivilized" because they reject a civilized status by violating the expectations for women in their particular social contexts. Judith, in *No Country for Young Men*, murders Sparky Driscoll, an American who threatens to expose financial improprieties of the rebels. Her great-niece, Gráinne, has love affairs and briefly leaves her husband, going to a women's shelter. Fleur, in *Tracks*, plays poker better than men, engages in flagrant sexual activity with Eli and has a strange relationship with a water monster. Pauline, in *Tracks*, has a baby then becomes a fanatical nun and murders her former lover because she mistakes him for the water monster. Delia, in *Delia's Song*, is involved in the Chicano student strike at Berkeley and years later has an impulsive sexual encounter in her friend Mattie's garden. The unconventional relationships that these women have with the men in their lives challenge the romanticization of women. Selwyn Langley, in *Myal*, fails to transform Ella O'Grady into a white Irish woman, as modeled on Rochester's attempt to make Jane Eyre into a lady. James wants Gráinne and her great-aunt Judith to resemble the women of Irish myth but his efforts to explore their secret knowledge ends in his death. Fleur is viewed mythically by some characters in *Tracks*, but she is only human and is ultimately unable to protect her family or her land. Delia discourages any romanticization of her relationship with Jeff by insisting that he read her manuscript, which reveals everything about her life.

The women characters in these four novels embody the mingling of genes and cultures inherent under colonialism. The Irish are a heterogeneous ethnic group characterized by the mingling of various peoples, including Vikings, Celts, Normans and British, through a history of successive invasions. Delia as Mexican American combines Indian and Spanish ancestry. *Myal*'s Ella O'Grady is a mixture of at least Irish and African ancestry. Pauline in *Tracks* is metis or "mixed blood" (Erdrich 1989: 14). In these novels we find the Irish presence everywhere as well as the influence of the colonizer's religions, especially Catholicism. Forced to emigrate or police imperial outposts because of the impact of British colonialism that dispossessed them of their land, the Irish in the New World are both colonizer and colonized. Ella O'Grady's father is an Irish policeman assigned to Jamaica under the British empire. One of the mixed race families in Tracks has an Irish surname, Morrissey, which means "taboo of the sea," thus suggesting their connection to Matchimanito Lake, a place of native power. In Delia's Song, Delia meets a man dressed as James Joyce for a Day of the Dead party. The nineteenth-century famine and the Irish diaspora that resulted dispersed the Irish to various regions of the world, notably North America, where they often mingled with Native Americans, African Americans and Mexican Americans.

As I began writing about these novels, I was caught in the dilemma of deciding on my position in relation to this narrative. It would have been dishonest to erase myself completely because this was at least partly a personal mission of recovering my history. Yet without some distance I felt drawn into the maelstrom of real pain present in these novels. Can we as readers or critics risk being pulled into an engagement with the experiential reality of the text? Toni Morrison has explicitly stated that her narrative strategy in Beloved is intentionally disorienting to her readers in order to provide an experience evocative of the vulnerability and confusion of those abducted from their homes and sold into slavery: "The reader is snatched, yanked, thrown into an environment completely foreign," so that he or she might actually experience what it would be like to be "snatched just as the slaves were from one place to another, from any place to another, without preparation and without defense" (Morrison 1989: 32).

In her article, "Fiction in the Scientific Procedure," Erna Brodber explains her decision to write novels about the colonial experience although she is a social scientist. Because social science is performed by outsiders and usually pursued with accountability to fellow academics rather than to the cultures and people being studied, Brodber decided that "writing through my feelings before entering the field was a valid methodological device" that enabled her to better understand the psychological repercussions of the African diaspora—the "relationship between history, tradition and defense mechanisms" (Brodber 1990: 167). Thus in writing her novels, she refuses the position of detached observer and becomes accountable to ordinary people:

My examination of Jamaican society could not be written from the standpoint of the objective outside observer communicating to disinterested scholars. It had to incorporate my "I" and to be presented in such a way that the social workers I was training saw their own "I" in the work. (Brodber 167)

Like Erna Brodber, who is a sociologist as well as novelist, I can occupy the objective and potentially colonizing space of an academic because of my educational privilege and my ability to theorize upon the silence of others, including my ancestors. When I experience resistance to writing through my personal past, it is as much from fear of revisiting my own Caliban, the postfamine Irish diaspora, as from fear of becoming Prospero. Literary critic Jane Tompkins believes that the imposed public-private dichotomy is a foundation of female oppression and resents the pretense that academic discourse is more exalted than conversation that is relevant to one's personal life.

You have to pretend that epistemology, or whatever you're writing about, has nothing to do with your life. The problem is that you can't talk about your private life in the course of doing your professional work. (Tompkins 1987: 169)

Alison Jagger, in "Love and Knowledge: Emotion in Feminist Epistemology," also questions the possibility of dispassionate objective knowledge. Jagger suggests that the myth of objectivity serves dominant groups, especially white men. Hegemonic social values that represent the values of the dominant group are naturalized and made to appear as social norms rather than social constructs. The myth of objectivity maintains the alliance of knowledge with power and its function in the domination of nature as well as the domination of oppressed groups through imperialism, racism and misogyny. This myth justifies silencing women, people of color and other oppressed groups, who are perceived as more subjective and "irrational." Jaggar believes that these oppressed groups offer the greatest potential for envisioning a more equitable society because they experience "outlaw" emotions that contest social norms such as racism, sexism, homophobia, greed, aggression and cruelty to animals. In these four novels about women from oppressed cultures, oral and folk traditions represent this subaltern, "outlaw" voice that speaks a passionate alternative to the dominant history.

My awareness of the difficulty and the politics of maintaining objectivity emerged when my writing about *Myal* coincided with the hurricane of August 1992 that passed through south Florida. The external reality of this hurricane not only resembled the violent storm caused by Ella's healing in the novel but also expressed my inner state as I allowed the novel to exorcise my repressed ghosts. Because my parents died during my childhood, my elderly aunt in south Florida was the only remaining family member who could supply information to fill in the gaps of my history. The realization of her fragile mortality made me recognize the importance of asking her for any memories that might allow me to retrace my origins. My father, who died when I was an infant, claimed that his mother was Native American but I have never been able to ascertain my ancestry with certainty. After my father's death, my mother and I lived in my grandmother's home. Granny was born in the nineteenth century and her parents apparently emigrated from Ireland some years after the famine of 1845–1852. As a child I remember hearing stories about the poverty of Ireland that forced my great-grandparents' emigration to Canada by steerage.

During this difficult period in my writing, I had two dreams concerning my ambiguous ancestry. In one dream, I'm in a classroom preparing to give a talk and Carolyn Heilbrun, author of *Reinventing Womanhood*, starts to write my introduction on the blackboard in ogham, an archaic Celtic script. She writes that my birthday is on Halloween and explains that this is the day when the Celtic year renews—a threshold between the worlds of the living and the dead. She tells me that I must inform the audience who I am and how painful it is to be in exile from Ireland. In the next dream, which occurred a short time later, I'm in a house with my mother. Somehow I had forgotten that she is still alive, and I'm glad because now she can explain the mystery surrounding my paternal grandmother. Then an elderly woman, apparently Native American, enters the room and I assume this must be my Native American grandmother, but my mother tells me that she is my Irish grandmother. I am again disappointed that there will be no explanation of my paternal family history.

Recently, I have begun to understand that because of the stories told to me about my ancestors' emigration, I had framed the loss of my maternal grandmother at the age of nine in terms of the losses of family, culture and community experienced by the Irish people as a consequence of the famine and diaspora. The parallel is relevant, although my framing of it was an unconscious part of my mourning process. When my grandmother died, an entire way of life abruptly vanished for me. Her death was the end of the extended family, including my mother and myself, that had shared her home. Most of my grandmother's possessions, objects of my childhood memories, seemed to suddenly disappear, even the garden that she had lovingly tended was allowed to wither. Only later, when finally visiting Ireland, did I recognize that our home was a microcosm of Irish culture in myriad ways, from the food to our regular attendance at wakes. When my grandmother died, I lost this cultural cocoon as well as her, which resembles the sudden loss of home and culture that occurred in late nineteenth-century Ireland due to the famine. To me this loss signifies the role that women like my grandmother play in cultural reproduction, passing on family and community stories and traditions.

As illustrated in the second opening quote, women and natives have been theorized upon in order to construct the identity of men and the colonizers. Eavan Boland writes about male Irish poets who used women—Kathleen Ní Houlihan, Dark Rosaleen—as motifs in their poems to construct an iconography of Irish national identity. Boland feels that this ornamental use of mythic women is dishonest to the reality of Irish women's lives and to the "wrath and grief of Irish history," which includes the dispossession of the native Irish from their land, culture and language that intensified with Cromwell's conquest in the seventeenth century (Boland 1989: 12).

The United States policy of using reservations to relocate and control Native Americans was modeled on Cromwell's plan for containment of the Irish.[2] In both situations, removal made land available to the colonizer and perhaps protected him from a contaminating contact with the colonized. For those subjected to removal, the result was the breakdown of traditional communal values through forced dispossession, relocation and impoverishment. Even before the nineteenth-century famine, there was a huge gap between the now landless Irish peasants and the prosperous, often absentee, English landlord class, who owned vast plantations and had power over their tenants to raise rents and evict those who couldn't pay. Elizabeth Smith, a landowner's wife, visited a woman who had miscarried from hard work and who lived in an old cow-house without windows. She described this scene in 1842, three years before the potato blight and subsequent famine: "I saw no bedclothes, straw below, a sort of old dark pot above; . . . four starved looking children, very clean, the poor fainting woman hardly able to speak and not able to raise herself" (Litton 1994: 11).

These subsistence conditions worsened when a blight destroyed the potato crop in 1845 and the British government failed to recognize promptly the seriousness of the crisis and thereby prevent widespread famine. The major emigration of the Irish occurred during and after the period of the 1845–1852 famine. This diaspora spread the Irish around the world, especially to North America and Australia. Anticipating the one hundred and fiftieth anniversary of the famine, John Waters of the *Irish Times* wrote an article entitled "Confronting the Ghost of our Past" about the tendency of the Irish to repress the history of the nineteenth-century famine and diaspora while unconsciously passing on the painful memories to their children. Waters mentions Sinéad O'Connor's song "Famine," which addresses the traumatic impact of the famine on the Irish and the need to remember and grieve what was lost.

There are parallels to this painful history in all four of the novels, as is more fully developed in their respective chapters. Jamaica, the setting of

Myal, has a history of the middle passage and slavery. Even after slavery ended, the former slaves continued to live precarious lives of poverty as landless peasants. Colonization of peoples' minds was resisted ideologically by religions like Myalism and oppression was resisted physically by slave uprisings and later by strikes. Native American nations like the Anishinaabeg in *Tracks* experienced displacement, dispossession and disruption of their cultures as Europeans moved into their homelands. "Within its boundaries the United States warred against native peoples and guaranteed political settlements for military alliances, the sale of lands, acquiescence to the reservation system, and the surrender of mineral rights" (Lincoln 1985: 18–19). The Anishinaabeg were decimated by disease and the cultural breakdown described in *Tracks,* as many lost their lands through the allotment policy. In 1848 the United States appropriated Northern Mexico, an area that now includes Texas, New Mexico and Arizona, and dispossessed the native Mexican inhabitants. The 1848 Treaty of Guadalupe Hidalgo, which established the new United States border at the Rio Grande and Gila rivers, guaranteed former Mexicans their property and civil rights but "like all of the treaties and agreements with the Indians, became mere paper when the matter at issue was land ownership" (Moquin 1972: 252). *Delia's Song* addresses the consequences of second-class citizenship for Mexican Americans, including job discrimination, deaths from drugs and the Vietnam War and obstacles to obtaining an education.

Studies about the psychological difficulties among survivors of the Holocaust can be applied to survivors of other similarly traumatic events in terms of lives lost and near genocide of an entire people and culture. For Holocaust survivors, the experience of losing or being separated from close family members was the most terrible aspect of the event. This also was experienced during the slave trade, the nineteenth-century Irish famine and the postconquest genocide of Native Americans. Consequences of the past, including unemployment and poverty that can lead to alcoholism or drug addiction as a response to hopelessness, continue into the present.

The abusive and degrading colonial relationship often resulted in self-negation and thus social and psychological problems for the colonized peoples. Scheper-Hughes, who made a study of the high rates of schizophrenia in rural Ireland, found similarities between the drinking of the rural Irish and the Pueblo Indians. She quotes a Pueblo man to whom she was showing her piece on rural Ireland: "Now this is like what is happening to us here. . . .You wouldn't have to scratch very deep to find the same hurt, the same loss and anger, and the drinking, always the drinking" (Scheper-Hughes 1987: 61). As a graduate student at the University of Chicago, Rosario Morales describes her drinking as a response to the scholarly requirement of maintaining distance from the painful histories of conquest that had impacted her ancestors. Morales realized that she was at the university to be a scholar and an anthropologist and therefore "not there to care that I was a Puerto Rican, a child of Taino Indians, of Spaniards, of African slaves. . . . Certainly not there to cry. No wonder I drank. . . . A soundless litany of death by exploration, of death by pacification, of death by manifest destiny" (Morales and Levins Morales 1986: 64).

The intense pain of losing family members and community connections is represented in all four novels by the continued presence of the dead in the memory of the living. In *Tracks*, Nanapush fears that he and Fleur will become windigo because they are attached too much to the dead they have lost in the epidemic. Delia is suffering a form of soul loss because she has not mourned the death of her brothers and the death of her dreams. The dead surround Judith in *No Country for Young Men* because she is still living in the past of the Irish war for independence from Britain. Gráinne also is haunted, but by memories of the famine and the evidence of it in the faces of the contemporary poor. Ella's healing is a symbolic act that addresses the need to heal the collective pain of Jamaican history, which includes slavery and ongoing racism, as well as her personal pain.

These novels recognize the interrelationship of the personal and the sociopolitical. The major characters in these novels are women who are obviously struggling with their personal concerns in a sociocultural milieu which they occupy or to which they are politically committed. These female characters shape their identities through interaction with the social and historical forces with which they are involved, and the subjectivities they express are often collective, thoroughly embedded in family, community and culture, thus undermining the individualism on which both patriarchy and colonialism are founded. Delia's relationships with her women friends, Fleur's with Nanapush and Ella's with other resisting members of the community are as important as their relationships with biological family. Colonized women, who have often been doubly theoretically constructed as icons, can reclaim the space of authentic difference by remembering and passing on stories of women. The recovery of the repressed must occur both on the personal and on the social levels because colonialism and postcolonialism, which is often a less visible colonialism, operate through oppressive social, political and economic structures sustained by ideologies of racism and sexism. These ideologies of inferiority and subjugation have been internalized as were the bodily suffering and emotional pain of various experiential oppressions such as dispossession, poverty and the legacy of conquest and slavery.

"Postcolonial" (an ambiguous term because the consequences of colonialism and ongoing economic recolonization endure)[3] women authors like these four are aware of the demands of a liberation movement that is based on asserting a cultural or national identity but may reinscribe patriarchal values and often does not provide an opportunity for the expression of female identity or desire. All the female characters in these novels are struggling to give voice to a subjectivity outside patriarchal constructions of women, while they reclaim their cultural identities that colonialism has attempted to erase. In some cases, colonialism imposes Christianity and other European philosophies on people, forcing them to reject traditional indigenous beliefs as invalid superstitions. Yet the belief systems of indigenous cultures are methods for assigning meaning to apparently arbitrary events in a way that reinforces the social order and enables people to function as cohesive community members.

The Chipewyan are an Athapaskan people in Canada with beliefs about giant fish and otters that resemble the beliefs about Misshepeshu, the water monster, in *Tracks*. The community uses these beliefs to explain individual misfortunes. For example, one story tells of a man who, with some companions, made fun of this belief by throwing logs into a river where a giant otter was said to live. Those involved subsequently either died or suffered the death of family members, which was explained as "Nobiecho's continuing revenge" (Sharp 1987: 233). Similar observations were made by Conrad Arensberg about so-called superstitions among the rural Irish. Arensberg determines that a belief that fairy folk have stolen the "real" person or animal functions as an explanation for sudden illnesses among people or cattle. This method for handling and explaining emotionally disturbing events enforces acceptable behavior within the community.

Through the enactment of these beliefs in their community, individuals are encouraged to remember the reciprocity of their relations with each other, a reciprocity that allows them to survive in a world of frequent scarcity. Through colonization, the Irish culture experienced a breakdown of the traditional clan structure and the monastic system, which had provided care for the sick, old and the homeless. This breakdown left the population even more vulnerable to the food crisis and resulting famine caused by British economic policy in the nineteenth century.

The collapse of the clan structure removed an age-old support system in which they had a place, lowly though that may have been. The suppression of the monasteries meant that the poor, the sick and the elderly had now no avenue of escape from the harsh reality of deprivation. (O'Connor 1995: 25)

By representing the differences between the colonizer and the colonized as a metaphysical fact of life, colonialist literature serves to dehistoricize the colonized and justify the allegedly civilizing colonial intervention. "By allowing the European to denigrate the native in a variety of ways, by permitting an obsessive, fetishistic representation of the native's moral inferiority, the allegory also enables the European to increase, by contrast, the store of his own moral superiority" (JanMohamed 1986: 103). Setting up such a dichotomy between the supposedly inferior native and the "morally superior" colonizer leaves the colonized with little option other than self-negation. Colonialism imposes binary oppositions of good and evil, savage and civilized that are fundamental to its self-justification. "While the covert purpose is to exploit the colony's natural resources thoroughly and ruthlessly through the various imperialist material practices, the overt aim, as articulated by colonialist discourse, is to 'civilize' the savage" (JanMohamed 81).

While negating the valid social role of indigenous culture, the colonization process also violates the life force or spirit of the colonized. This explains not only the references to vampires in *No Country for Young Men* and *Delia's Song* and zombies and spirit thievery in *Myal* but even the genesis of the original story of Bram Stoker's *Dracula*, whose author was born in Dublin in 1847, the worst year of the famine. As a novel about the "anxiety of reverse colonization," *Dracula* represents the colonizer's guilt over the damage done to the colonized by British imperialism and the fear that the victim will retaliate. This retaliation is signified by Count Dracula's intent to pollute the blood of British women and thus transform them into vampires. Societies impose rituals of virginity on women in order to ensure paternity and therefore cultural purity. Vampirism, as a parody both of the sexual act and the maternal act of breast-feeding with a substitution of blood for milk, endangers the purity of women, whose bodily boundaries are important because of their role in reproduction.

We cannot possibly interpret rituals concerning excreta, breast milk, saliva and the rest unless we are prepared to see in the body a symbol of society, and to see the powers and dangers credited to social structure reproduced in small on the human body. (Douglas 1989: 115)

The purity of women is definitely an issue in *No Country for Young Men*, and James's "pollution" of Gráinne is one of the motives for Patsy's murder of her lover. In some of these novels, these pollution concerns are signified by racially mixed characters such as Pauline in *Tracks* and Ella in *Myal* and associated with the mestiza identity of Delia in *Delia's Song*. As is discussed later, contemporary Chicana feminists are revalidating women such as la Malinche, seen as the founder of a new consciousness rather than bearer of a polluted status because of her violation by Cortés. Gloria Anzaldúa's concept of "mestiza consciousness," a concept which applies to *Delia's Song*, also validates the mingling of genes and cultures in the Mexican people rather than attempting to reinstate an idealized past.

The novels under consideration demonstrate challenges to the hegemonic patriarchal and colonial orders through their expression of social structures, ritual processes and narrative techniques that validate flexibility, ambiguity and pollution. These novels convey this emphasis through the use of characters with fluid identities; through unconventional constructions of family and kinship and by situating the characters in hybrid cultural contexts. This zone of cultural contact and mingling of colonial and native symbolic systems has been designated "borderland" by Gloria Anzaldúa, a "vague and undetermined place created by the emotional residue of an unnatural boundary," such as the United States-Mexican border, that signifies a wound, "*una herida abierta* where the Third World grates against the first and bleeds . . . the lifeblood of two worlds merging to form a third country —a border culture" (Anzaldúa 1987: 3). Edward Brathwaite, a Jamaican scholar, explains his concept of creolization or cultural contact: "Here in Jamaica, fixed within the dehumanizing institution of slavery, were two cultures of people, having to adapt themselves to a new environment and to each other. The friction created by this confrontation was cruel, but it was also creative" (Brathwaite 1971: 307). Similarly, Richard Kearney recognizes the ambiguity of Irish identity, especially as it encompasses the Irish diaspora.

The Irish thing surfaces, almost in spite of oneself, when the obsession with a unique identity is abandoned. . . . Now as we are rediscovering ourselves through our encounter with others, reclaiming our voice in our migrations through other cultures and continents—Europe, Britain, North America. (Kearney 1988: 187)

These descriptions of border, mestiza or creole zones of colonial contact and the resulting hybrid identities recall Victor Turner's definition of liminality.[4] Originally "liminal" referred to a phase in rites of passage as delineated by Arnold van Gennep. The three phases are "separation, margin (or limen, signifying 'threshold' in Latin), and aggregation" (Turner 1969: 94). The liminal phase is the state in which the ritual subject has an ambiguous status before being reintegrated into the community with a new identity. Liminality is betwixt and between the structures of social order, thus it is "frequently likened to death, to being in the womb, to invisibility, to darkness, to bisexuality, to the wilderness, and to an eclipse of the sun or moon" (Turner 95).

Liminality is disturbing because it destabilizes authority and evokes an uncanny site that is constructed from a bricolage of disparate fragments, thus returning the participant to the threshold of birth or rebirth associated with the mother's genitals. "It often happens that male patients declare that they feel there is something uncanny about female genital organs. This *unheimlich* place, however, is the entrance to the former *heim* [home] of all human beings" (Freud 1919: 399). The *unheimlich* is suggested by the paradoxical and ambivalent Celtic *sheela-na-gig*, which signifies the maternal body and thus Freud's pre-oedipal state that precedes a symbolic order. The *sheela-na-gig*, which shows a woman exposing her devouring genitals, has been found on churches in Ireland and England and suggests that the *unheimlich* place of birth is also the source of death. This symbol was used on a controversial counterhegemonic Dublin Millennium poster of 1987 called "The Spirit of Woman," which was created in response to the official Millennium poster, "Faces of Dublin," in which every face was male.

Molly Mullin, in "Representations of History, Irish Feminism, and the Politics of Difference," thinks that the *sheela-na-gig* and the controversy that it inspired is instructive because of the challenge it presents to hegemonic representations of Irish history. By its simultaneous celebration of female genitalia and representation of death as the inevitable outcome of birth, the sheela destabilizes the notion that sexuality and death can be separated. The icon acquired an especially subversive quality when journalist Nell McCafferty used the sheela wearing a nun's veil to criticize ignorance of the female body and sexuality in Catholic-dominated Ireland. Mullin compares its impact to John and Jean Comaroff's description of a Tswana madman, wearing the initials of the South African Railways on his chest and carrying a bishop's miter made from black plastic garbage bags, which ironically subverts the dual colonialisms of industrial capitalism and missionary religion. "Like madmen and witches everywhere, he offered genteel society an image of itself that it would rather forget" (Comaroff quoted in Mullin 1991: 49).

When the four women authors in my investigation affirm female subjectivity, they do not attempt to erase this *unheimlich* space of origins. The female characters in their novels inhabit cultural border zones and psychological threshold states. The ambiguous position of the colonized women characters in these novels is signified as an uncanny threshold between life and death. There are references to Halloween as a metaphor for liminality in *No Country for Young Men* and to the Day of the Dead, its Mexican equivalent, in *Delia's Song*. Victor Turner discusses the significance of Halloween as a time for an alliance between "the innocent and the wicked, children and witches, who purge the community" (Turner 1969: 183). This might apply to the childlike Patsy and Judith, who purge their community of threatening outsiders in *No Country for Young Men*. Delia's masquerade at the Day of the Dead party enables her to initiate sex with a stranger. "The Halloween children exemplify several liminal motifs: their masks insure them anonymity, for no one knows just whose particular children they are. But . . . anonymity here is for purposes of aggression" (Turner 172).

Each of the novels addresses the colonial influence that situates the characters betwixt and between cultures and often in states of consciousness that are betwixt and between life and death. The characters in *No Country for Young Men*, especially Judith, are caught in a time zone that encompasses the era of the Irish civil war in the 1920s as well as the renewal of the troubles in the 1970s. There are references to both bogs and fairy mounds, which have liminal characteristics and thus the potential for enabling a reversal of repression and colonization. Transcending limits of space and time, the Other World could be "reached through a cave, the waters of a lake, a magic mist, or simply through the acquisition of heightened insight" (Mac Cana 1987: 314).

Delia exists in a betwixt and between state that can be compared to *susto*, a condition of soul loss according to Mexican folk culture, because she has experienced many losses but she finally begins to awaken to life through her sexual encounter with a man disguised as James Joyce at a Day of the Dead party. *Myal* describes the colonization of Ella's mind as created by the texts of a colonial education, especially the works that dichotomize colonized and colonizer, such as Kipling's poem about the "white man's burden" and Shakespeare's *The Tempest*. This binary representation of colonized and colonizer as opposites is particularly troubling for Ella because she is half black and half white, thus her body, associated with her Jamaican mother, is split from her mind associated with her Irish father and with the colonial symbolic order he enforces. Ella's zombified state resulting from this split is finally healed by the Myal man. The three main characters in *Tracks*, Fleur, Pauline and Nanapush, are also survivors of personal and cultural loss who feel very close to the dead and can even cross over into that realm. Their liminality is due both to grieving these losses and to being caught in a world betwixt their Anishinaabeg culture and the encroachment of European culture. Their survival is negotiated by their ability to use trickster strategies and elude categorization.

These women characters use the life-death threshold or the living death of *susto* or zombification to illuminate the ambiguity of inhabiting a world that is in-between cultures and to affirm identities as hybrid and complex subjects. These threshold states are associated with the release of repressed emotions of grief, rage and demonic madness as transformative energies with which these characters can rebirth themselves. Liminal zones are complicated and unstable sites of cultural contact and painful loss that offer the female characters an opportunity to descend into the abyss of nonbeing and reconstruct a more authentic identity through their rites of passage. Through this crossing of thresholds, the madness and schizophrenic manicheanism of colonialism is transformed into a vehicle for rites of passage into a new identity, a complex subjectivity which can express this interrelation of the personal and historical. With the multidimensional meaning of these texts, the authors challenge the socially constructed symbolic order imposed on them under colonialism and embrace a cultural and linguistic ambiguity that challenges that binary order.

The prevalence of themes of loss and madness in postcolonial literature illustrates an awareness that colonialism encompasses experiences of loss—home, family and culture. However, loss and madness can be reclaimed as counterhegemonic forces. The motif of madness can signify this encounter between the oppressive colonial order and the return of its repressed precolonial culture. Employed as a narrative strategy, fragmentary or "irrational" discourse can represent a resistance to colonial or patriarchal mastery. Rational control is subverted by eruptions of repressed stories and traditions from the unconscious or supernatural realm to subvert control of the "rational" hegemonic discourse. The gaps in the fragmentary recovery of lost stories can be an effective means of destabilizing a reinscription of the hegemony.

NOTES

1. I will not attempt to summarize the vast amount of recent work in this area but will refer the reader to several resources: M. Jacqui Alexander and Chandra Talpade Mohanty, eds., *Feminist Genealogies, Colonial Legacies, Democratic Futures*; and Sandra Kumamoto Stanley, ed., *Other Sisterhoods: Literary Theory and U.S. Women of Color*. These two useful anthologies have introductions that provide background relevant to issues of theory and voice and that problematize constructs, such as "women of color." See especially Marie Anna Jaimes Guerrero, "Civil Rights versus Sovereignty: Native American Women in Life and Land Strug-

gles" and Honor Ford-Smith, "Ring Ding in a Tight Corner: Sistren, Collective Democracy, and the Organization of Cultural Production," both in *Feminist Genealogies*. Other sources relevant to discussions of specific literatures include: Anthony Bradley and Maryann Gialanella Valiulis, eds., *Gender and Sexuality in Modern Ireland*; D. Letticia Galindo and Maria Dolores Gonzales, eds., *Speaking Chicana: Voice, Power and Identity*; and Joy Harjo and Gloria Bird, eds., *Reinventing the Enemy's Language*.

2. For parallels between colonization of Ireland and the New World, see Nicholas P. Canny, "The Ideology of English Colonization: From Ireland to America" and Nicholas P. Canny, *The Elizabethan Conquest of Ireland*.

3. The post in postcolonial "belies both the continuities and discontinuities of power that have shaped the legacies" of the imperial powers and suspends us in an "historically empty space . . . a perpetual present marked only as 'post' " (McClintock 1992: 87, 97). Postcolonial can become a "universalizing category which neutralizes significant geopolitical differences" and obfuscates the continuity of first world hegemony, neocolonialism and anticolonial struggles (Shohat 1992: 103).

4. Though hybridity can be useful in reversing racist colonial and idealistic anticolonial notions of purity, Shohat advises against embracing the concept without qualifications. "Post-colonial theory's celebration of hybridity risks an anti-essentialist condescension toward those communities obliged by circumstances to assert, for their very survival, a lost and even irretrievable past" (Shohat 110).

2
∽ *Tracks* ∽

In Louise Erdrich's *Tracks* (1989), as in all four of these novels, the characters are shaped by the historical context that they inhabit. A central event in this novel is the rape of Fleur, which signifies on an individual level the rape of Anishinaabeg land and culture on a collective level. The novel's personal events are framed by the larger context, including the breakdown of community and loss of land when the Turcot Lumber Company pressures people to sell land to them, causing conflict between those who want to sell and those who resist. Foreclosure on allotments of those who can't pay their annual fees has increased the pressure on tribal members to sell their land. When Father Damien shows Nanapush and others the map of reservation lands, they see that the lands lost to the tribe are marked pink. To Nanapush in particular the spreading pink area on the map has disturbing implications.

Fleur's rape by white men early in the novel is symbolically reenacted at the novel's end with the rape of the woods on her land. Through her trickster dance of illusion, Fleur redefines both "rapes," but she is nevertheless unable to prevent the violation of her body and her land by white men. Pauline, a mixed blood and one of the novel's two narrators, overhears but can't stop Fleur's rape. She later locks the perpetrators in the freezer, killing two of them and permanently injuring the third. Fleur and Pauline are alike in the sense that each tries separately and individually to save their Anishinaabeg people, although Pauline thinks they will be saved by accepting Christianity and white culture while Fleur tries to preserve the land and traditional culture.

At the beginning of Louise Erdrich's novel, Fleur, Pauline and Nanapush, the three main characters, are the sole survivors of their families, who died during smallpox and tuberculosis epidemics. During the course of the novel, these characters experience additional losses of people, land and culture. Yet by the novel's end, it is clear that these three are not the end of their family lines because they have produced descendants. Fleur and Pauline give birth to daughters Lulu and Marie, and Nanapush is a surrogate father to Fleur's daughter Lulu, giving her the surname Nanapush.

Thus although the novel opens with Nanapush's vanishing Indian discourse about the last buffalo, last bear and so forth, this rhetoric can be viewed as an example of Erdrich's use of "survival humor," an ironic humor that pervades the novel (Cotelli 1990: 46). The use of this "vanishing Indian" discourse by the self-acknowledged trickster Nanapush sets the background for *Tracks* and tempers with irony the novel's treatment of the serious issues of individual and cultural survival. *Track's* central characters inhabit a world that is in-between white and Anishinaabeg cultures.[1] The three main characters also inhabit the threshold region between life and death, which is perhaps indicative of their position as survivors who have lost their entire families and are experiencing a cultural crisis.

During the winter of death that decimates the Anishinaabeg, Nanapush rescues Fleur from the fever and starvation that has killed their families. He fears that their dead relatives may return if they allow their thoughts to dwell on them and, in fact, Nanapush and Fleur do become half *windigo* for awhile because they become filled with memories of the dead. "All insanities were termed *windigo*, after the mythology's giant cannibalistic skeleton of ice. . . . Psychically, the *windigo* disorder involved projection of the sufferer's fears and vindictiveness, besides the experiences or anxious anticipations of starvation" (Landes 1986: 13). In contemporary terms, *windigo* might be called posttraumatic stress disorder, an experience of severe anxiety that overwhelms those who have survived traumas, including widespread death in their community, whether from starvation, disease or war. Later when her newborn arrives too early and is threatened with death, Fleur enters the world of the dead to rescue her.

Pauline follows Fleur across this threshold, recognizing her mother and father along the path, and watches Fleur play cards to gamble for the soul of her infant. While there, Fleur learns that her daughter, Lulu, is also endangered. She is able to save only Lulu and her failure to save the unnamed infant breaks Fleur's heart and her spirit. "Fleur heard her vanished child in every breath of wind" (Erdrich 1989: 170). Once again she has survived while others die but this survival of her child's death seems unbearable to Fleur. After this loss, Fleur is unable to produce food for her family or to empower her lover Eli's hunting and fishing.

Toward the novel's end, Nanapush once again feels overwhelmed by memories of his painful losses. This world of the dead does not frighten Nanapush because it promises a reunion with loved ones. Yet he once again resists the attraction of joining his family because he chooses to remain with the living, especially Fleur and her daughter Lulu, whom he has named Lulu Nanapush for the child he lost, "[o]ur small daughter, Moskatikinaugun, Red Cradle, whom I'd called Lulu" (Erdrich, 220).

Like the other survivors, Pauline is attracted to this world of the dead, but unlike them she often seems more in love with death than with life. In fact if attachment to one's children is a sign of attachment to life, it is significant that Pauline totally rejects her child because she decides the baby was conceived in sin, both the sin of sexuality and the sin of being Indian. Pauline defines herself as a scavenger who has an aptitude for midwiving people into death rather than into life. To Pauline, death is a "form of grace." Once she discovers her ability to cut the thread that attaches the dying to life, Pauline feels a great relief from the torment of guilt she has suffered since Fleur's rape and her role in murdering the rapists.

Although most studies on the psychology of genocide survivors are of Jews who survived the Nazi Holocaust, there are many parallels between the psychological response of Jewish Holocaust survivors and the responses of Erdrich's characters. The Nazi Holocaust was a major psychological trauma for the survivors because they lost not only families and communities but also an entire people and culture. "The quantity or the quality of losses may be beyond one's capacity to integrate, e.g., when in the case of the Holocaust one's entire people and civilization perished. But even if we were to discount these difficulties, which could fill volumes, we still come back to the simplest, most basic fact that there are limitations to the kind of losses an individual may be able to deal with through mourning" (Krystal 1991: 104).

Henry Krystal enumerates the psychological consequences for the survivors. There is often considerable guilt over being a survivor when so many others have died, especially in the case of those who lost a child or spouse. "Their survivor guilt becomes severe, and some of these individuals assume a depressive or penitent lifestyle" (Krystal 95). There is often reluctance to remember and reconcile with the past because it would necessitate reexperiencing the feelings of helplessness and shame associated with having to submit to a fate imposed on one by others. This is reminiscent of the shame that could be associated with being a rape victim like Fleur and yet it is Pauline, as witness, who seems to feel this shame most profoundly. Other responses noted by Krystal include "continuing the victim identity," feeling rage and "righteous indignation" and creating a "mythology of heroic resistance" (Krystal 104–5). All of these characteristics can be recognized to some degree in Erdrich's characters. Pauline often seems trapped in the victim role and adopts a penitent lifestyle, while Fleur is almost equally trapped in her myth of heroic resistance and is devastated by the death of her infant when she fails in her heroic role.

Survivors may choose to become numb, resulting in a loss of aliveness, rather than feel unbearable pain. Yet only those who are able to stop repressing the painful memories and negotiate a mourning process are eventually able to truly love and feel alive again. This avoidance of painful memories could explain Pauline's preference for death over life; her fear of feeling her body despite the sexual desire that still burns in her; and especially her religious asceticism and masochism, which she expresses through self-imposed deprivations—wearing potato sacks, not washing, and denying her need to eat and even to urinate. In fact, her adoption of a masochistic version of Catholicism coincides with another characteristic of survivors, which is to embrace rigid religious beliefs, in her case a manichean view of the battle between good and evil represented by the conflict between the two symbolic systems, Anishinaabeg and Christian.

The actual destruction of basic trust which resulted from the events of the Holocaust makes true faith and trust in the benevolence of an omnipotent God impossible. So, the yearning for the comfort of religion only results in a piling up of rituals. (Krystal 108)

As with Holocaust survivors, the survivors in *Tracks* are coping with the loss of an entire way of life. Authors of *Native American Postcolonial Psychology*, Eduardo and Bonnie Duran, who apply the theory of posttraumatic stress disorder to the impact of the conquest on Native Americans, accuse traditional psychology of neocolonialism because it imposes a Euro-American subjectivity on colonized peoples. Referring to literature on Holocaust survivors and intergenerational posttraumatic stress disorder, the Durans believe that the 500 years of conquest during which Europeans have attempted to subjugate, exterminate, assimilate and oppress native peoples has resulted in self-hatred, alcoholism, suicide and domestic violence. Citing Frantz Fanon, they advocate that formerly colonized peoples, in particular Native Americans, define themselves in terms of indigenous knowledge systems not through the logical positivism of European thought.

Initial contact disrupted the traditional "lifeworld" with spirituality at its core. This was later compounded by relocation to reservations and removal of children to boarding schools, which resulted in overwhelming grief. However, the traditional belief systems that could heal this loss also had often been destroyed. In the case of the Anishinaabeg, the values of the dominant American system, which is based on private ownership of land and the power of money, have replaced belief in the power of the *manitos*, "spirit prototypes of plants, birds, beasts, elemental forces, and life circumstances such as Poverty and Motherhood" (Landes 1986: 22). The *manitos* are guardian spirits or supernatural beings who were sought as helpers through a vision quest. In Anishinaabeg stories collected during 1893–1895, it was recorded that water serpents had deserted a lake that they once inhabited. "The Indians think that the reason that the serpents have gone away is that they do not like the whites, whom the serpents believe to be as strong as themselves" (Bourgeois 1994: 47).

Nanapush repeatedly makes references to the importance of belief, especially consensual belief, in the construction of reality. He knows that the community's fear of Fleur is related to their beliefs about her, based on the gossip they heard and believed. He mentions the power of belief again when he describes Fleur's loss of belief in herself because she was unable to save her baby, who was born too soon, or to save her land. Nanapush regards Fleur's problem as a tendency to confuse the power that works through her and is beyond her control with a power that she owns and controls. Another manifestation of the crisis of belief is evidenced by Pauline's extreme response of abandoning her traditional beliefs for Christianity and imagining herself to be entirely white because she believes that the whites are more powerful.

Often, times of crisis result in the development of a new religious cult, such as the Ghost Dance of the Plains peoples and the Midewiwin among the Anishinaabeg. The Midewiwin began as a medicine rite designed to "purge Ojibwa society of the ills, both physical and psychological, associated with European contact" (Brehm 1996: 691). Loss of shared belief is only one aspect of the breakdown of cohesion in the Anishinaabeg community. "Prior to the white man's arrival, the Chippewas had no such practice as individual ownership of land. Fishing and hunting grounds, maple groves, and rice fields were common property" (Danziger 1977: 11). When the Anishinaabeg people lived traditionally as a seminomadic woodland people, they accepted famine as a continual threat yet during these times of hardship, famine was often avoided because of the cooperative spirit of the people, which ensured that those who had surpluses would share with the needy. During a famine, Fleur realizes that she is unable to use her power to assist Eli's hunting and fishing skills, and Margaret, Eli's mother, finally goes to town to obtain government relief rations, complaining that this wouldn't have happened among her family because they "stick together" (Erdrich 1989: 172).

Margaret's statement reflects the novel's context of white encroachment, population and land loss, and community breakdown, thus implicitly contrasting the fragile Anishinaabeg ethos that ensured survival with the postconquest collapse of this ethos resulting in increasing risk to survival. People who have lost the sense of security that comes from shared prosperity and shared beliefs are then more vulnerable to the apparent power of money-based white civilization. During the late nineteenth century, the Bureau of Indian Affairs (BIA) pressured the Anishinaabeg to convert from their nomadic woodland lifestyle to a sedentary agricultural lifestyle. Of course, this pressure would also cause individual and collective identity crises because their religious belief system was integrated with their economic and social system. "Allotment was only a first step. The Chippewas were then strongly encouraged to farm their small tracts and become self-supporting as soon as possible . . . it seemed that the time had come when the red man must farm or starve" (Danziger 1977: 98).

Danziger observes that harvesting the lumber on the reservation served multiple purposes. Not only did this lumber serve to meet the increased demand for homes and barns as white settlers moved westward, but it also removed the obstacle to converting the Anishinaabeg to an agricultural lifestyle. The BIA felt that the continued existence of these pine and hardwood forests on the reservations only prolonged the traditional woodland culture, which was detrimental to the spread of American culture and progress among the Anishinaabeg. Fleur, whose consciousness is inaccessible to the reader, is an anomaly primarily because she clings to a traditional Anishinaabeg worldview and to her woodland, living in the "old days" despite the increasingly predominant capitalist privatization of land (Erdrich 1989: 174).

Clifford Geertz, in "Ethos, World View and the Analysis of Sacred Symbols," describes the holistic nature of religion and culture in a manner that explains why the collapse of a cultural belief system would be personally and collectively devastating. A belief system plays an important role in supporting social values that give meaning to reality as experienced in that culture. "The need for such a metaphysical grounding for values seems to vary quite widely in intensity from culture to culture and from individual to individual, but the tendency to desire some sort of factual basis for one's commitments seems practically universal" (Geertz 1973: 131). In *Tracks* Louise Erdrich presents the reader with narratives told by Pauline and Nanapush, each of whom offers different perspectives on Anishinaabeg history and on Fleur Pillager, a controversial transgressive woman of power in a community which has been decimated by the Dawes Allotment Act and finally by disease. Through these two perspectives, Erdrich presents Anishinaabeg beliefs as being just as valid as Christian or Euro-American beliefs about life, death and the supernatural.

By relativizing these conflicting epistemologies or worldviews, Erdrich encourages the reader to experience life from the marginalized position of Native Americans who inhabit a threshold space in-between the dominant culture and their traditional cultures. For example, Nanapush complains about white-imposed ideas of measurement and boundaries and the "separation of experience into real and imagined events, and of time into past, present, and future, [as] . . . part of an alien and oppressive world view which, together with writing, makes communication extremely difficult" (Rainwater 1990: 418). According to Catherine Rainwater, Erdrich presents her readers with the relativity of the novel's various systems of meaning or "conflicting codes," as she calls them, that include:

- Christianity versus shamanic religion;
- mechanical or industrial time versus ceremonial time;
- the nuclear family versus tribal kinship systems;
- main or privileged characters versus characters of equal status;
- privileged narrative voices as opposed to dialogical or polyphonic narrative development. (Rainwater 406–7)

Erdrich relativizes these worldviews by representing them through the three main characters, who function as tricksters. The trickster myth is found among most cultures, from ancient Greece to contemporary African and Native American peoples. Nanapush is named for Naanabozho, Anishinaabeg culture-hero and trickster who "was known to take on many forms and many personalities within a single myth . . . a composite synthetic figure" (Vecsey 1983: 85). There are female tricksters as well as male, and the customary representation of trickster as a "priapean male, dominated by his sexual appetites" may be the result of a bias by male ethnographers (Wiget 1990: 89). In *Tracks*, Pauline, Fleur and Nanapush all have the trickster's strong libidos, and they occupy threshold realms between animal and human as well as between life and death.

Fleur is represented as a shaman, a person possessing access to supernatural power, through her transformation into a bear and through her connection with the ambiguous water monster Misshepeshu. "Micipijiu ('Misshepeshu' in Erdrich's work) was the great horned cat, the underwater lion, the night panther who could raise storms with a flick of his tail" (Brehm 1996: 677). Pauline and Nanapush also clearly possess supernatural power. Pauline practices "love medicine" on Eli and Sophie, projecting herself into Sophie's body to seduce Eli, and Nanapush can project himself into Eli's body and assist him in the hunt.

"Trickster is the image of man continually creating himself, never finishing the task of distinguishing through encounter the Me from the not-Me" (Wiget 1990: 21). Thus to separate Pauline from Nanapush and Fleur because she seems more negative and dangerous, preoccupied more with death than life and eros, would be to slip into a dichotomy that isn't relevant in the trickster worldview. The ambiguous character of most "literary marginals" confound this dichotomy between good and evil. "In contrast to this either/or approach, we might better view this ambiguity as a necessary dualism and define marginality as being outside or between the boundaries of dominant groups for better and for worse" (Babcock-Abrahams 1975: 150). The trickster transgresses boundaries into taboo regions of death and sexuality, realms that represent a dissolution of boundaries. Trickster's "beneficence, though central, results from the breaking of rules and the violating of taboos. . . . As a 'criminal' culture-hero, he embodies all possibilities—the most positive and the most negative—and is paradox personified" (Babcock-Abrahams 148).

Like Ella, in *Myal*, who creates a hurricane when she discharges the internalized colonial waste, Fleur is a force of nature that cannot be disembodied and reduced to a textual representation. Her passionate pleasures and anguish seem to overflow the page. She is both body and soul, bound to her traditional culture and closely connected to the land that has sustained her family and continues to be haunted by their ghosts. Her story is narrated alternately by Nanapush, a self-acknowledged trickster and by Pauline, whom Nanapush regards as a pathological liar, ergo also a trickster. It is primarily through the narrative of Pauline, a mixed blood who becomes a Catholic nun, that Fleur is represented as a dangerous and possibly evil figure. Pauline tries to spilt reality into rigid categories of good and evil. While the other narrator of Fleur's story, Nanapush, also represents Fleur as a transgressive medicine woman, he embraces ambiguity, whether of the sacred which is both healing and dangerous, or of human nature.

According to Pauline, Fleur can transform herself into a bear when hunting and has twice resisted abduction by Misshepeshu, the water man who lives in Matchimanito Lake. "These missionaries were never loons, never bears, their wives and mothers were never killdeers on the shoreline. We were animals and birds, even when we were converted and that was the difference between culture and civilization" (Vizenor 1984: 46). In *The Practice of the Wild*, Gary Snyder discusses a Tlinglit story, " The Woman Who Married a Bear," told by Maria Johns. In this story, the fluid boundaries between humans and animals are indicative of a relationship based on respectful reciprocity.

There's a world behind the world we see that is the same world but more open, more transparent, without blocks. Like inside a big mind, the animals and humans all can talk, and those who pass through here get power to heal and help. (Snyder 1990: 164)

Fleur is the incarnate reminder of a way of life temporarily submerged, like Misshepeshu, but not truly eradicated. She is a haunting presence and a dangerous woman. Fleur has twice resisted abduction by the supernatural Misshepeshu/ Micipijiu. "To resist him is to nullify his threat and to reinforce women's cultural power in a patrilineal, patriarchal society" because "Micipijiu is the embodiment of male sexuality from his projecting horns and sharp spines to his long pointed tail" (Brehm 1996: 686). Those humans who sought Micipijiu in a vision would be granted great powers to do both good and evil. Eli discovers Fleur's power when he and his mother let Fleur's land fees go unpaid in order to keep their land. After he rescues her from suicide and tries to caress her, Fleur grabs his ears and hisses a curse. Fleur endures through the stories of Nanapush and Pauline as both an isolated woman who could resist but not defeat the inevitable European occupation of native land and a mythical woman so full of unrepressed primal energy that she couldn't accept her limitations when confronted by the white people's economic power. When Nanapush goes to bury the Pillagers who died during the epidemic, he discovers that Fleur still lives and is "wild as a filthy wolf" (Erdrich 1989: 3).

While Nanapush describes Fleur's "animal" nature as a positive passionate energy, Pauline, embracing an ascetic Catholicism, associates this passionate life force with evil and the devil. She describes Fleur's raw power as dangerous, connecting it to the water serpent who suggests the devil to her, as Fleur suggests Eve and fallen human nature. As a child, Fleur nearly drowned in the lake but was saved by two men, who afterwards disappeared. At fifteen she again almost drowned but was washed up on shore.

According to Pauline, men avoided Fleur Pillager after the second near drowning because they realized that she was desired by Misshepeshu, whom Pauline describes as "a devil, that one . . . he sprouts horns, fangs, claws, fins" (Erdrich 11). She also endows Fleur with animal-like characteristics that Pauline believes imply something sinister and dangerous: "Fleur's shoulders were broad and curved as a yoke, her hips fishlike, slippery, narrow. . . . Her glossy braids were like the tails of animals" (Erdrich 18).

Contrary to Vizenor's and Snyder's positive descriptions of human-animal rapport, Pauline's descriptions of Fleur's animal-like qualities suggest the discourse of savagery versus civilization used by the Puritan settlers of America to justify their appropriation of land from the native inhabitants. Puritans believed these natives were savage because they did not dominate and exploit their natural environment, as divinely mandated in the Bible. "Aboriginal Americans, so English voyagers were again and again to find, denied their holy, human selves and lived like beasts; they were in the traditional terminology, more animal than rational" (Pearce 1988: 5). Eventually, as the natives offered resistance to their displacement by the settlers toward whom they had initially displayed hospitality, the Puritan discourse of savagism assumed an even more hostile tone. The uncivilized qualities of the natives were defined as a "sign of Satan's power" (Pearce 20). The native's possession of land by natural right was superseded by possession of land according to the laws of a civilized state and in accord with God's command to occupy the earth, increase, and multiply. "Wherever the Indian opposed the Puritan there Satan opposed God; Satan had possessed the Indian until he had become virtually a beast; Indian worship was devil worship" (Pearce 22).

In addition to her "savage" attributes, Fleur has other qualities that alienate her from the community but apparently the most transgressive attribute, from the perspective of white men, is her aptitude for gambling and her participation in the usually male card games with Lily, Dutch and Tor. After winning on one occasion, Fleur is apparently raped by the men. Since both narrators of Fleur's story are unreliable because of their trickster qualities, the reader cannot be certain of exactly what happened. This uncertainty contributes to the ambiguous origins of Lulu, the child born to Fleur the following spring. Was Lulu conceived during the alleged rape, or during the public erotic escapades with Eli or during visits to the water monster? Ultimately, Nanapush gives Lulu his name, thus confusing her paternity even more.

Fleur embodies an excess of libido or life force. Her two pregnancies are associated with passionate lovemaking with Eli. Nanapush had advised Eli on how to satisfy a woman by giving examples of the different tastes of his several wives. Eli's mother, Margaret, who hires a spy to observe the sexual encounters between Fleur and Eli, thinks they behave like animals, having sex outside in the grass and even in the trees. Later Nanapush himself describes the winter of love resulting in Fleur's second pregnancy, when sounds of pleasure were heard coming from the cabin, where Fleur and Eli were sequestered.

Ironically, Pauline herself is as dangerous and excessive as she imagines Fleur to be. Pauline's talent for death is the complement of Fleur's talent for eros and life. Yet she does not seem to recognize her representation of Fleur as a projection of that which she has tried to reject within herself. Pauline is paradoxical because, like Fleur, she has powerful libidinal energy which can be expressed in healing, sexuality or destructiveness. Unlike Fleur, she is a mixed blood, caught between traditional beliefs of the supernatural, for which she has an aptitude, and Catholicism, which she sees as a means of survival in the world that is replacing the Anishinaabeg reality. By embracing Catholicism, Pauline can repress her sexuality and sublimate it into a form of holy masochism.

Like Ella, in *Myal*, who becomes full of feces, and Judith, the nun in *No Country for Young Men*, who is smelly and abject, Pauline, who is dirty because she refuses to wash, signifies a return of the repressed. "Excrement and its equivalents (decay, infection, disease, corpse etc.) stand for the danger to identity that comes from without," a danger that threatens the social order (Kristeva 1982: 71). Pauline is an anomaly outside the social order because she is neither white nor Anishinaabeg and belongs nowhere because she has lost her family. Pauline like Ella and Judith has been brainwashed by the internalization of colonial ideologies that often denigrate the colonized. Like the Irish nationalists in O'Faolain's novel, for whom suffering is seen as necessary to survival in the context of Irish history, Pauline embraces suffering and denies the natural instincts that she considers sinful.

Yet despite this attempt at purifying herself, Pauline is literally the dirtiest person in the novel. After joining the convent, she ceases to wash or change clothes. Pauline's rejection of hygiene signifies that she is dirty in Mary Douglas's sense that dirt is matter out of place or the "rejected bits" that don't fit when order is imposed (Douglas 1989: 160). Of course since this is Pauline according to Nanapush, the self-avowed trickster is constantly destabilizing Pauline's narrative of Fleur by suggesting that Pauline is the dirty savage, not Fleur. Pauline as masochistic nun has neglected her hygiene and regards her stench as the odor of sanctity: "My rank aroma was the perfume my soul exuded, devotion's air" (Erdrich 1989: 153). Nanapush views it differently and tells Pauline, "You're more and more like the whites who never wash themselves clean!" (Erdrich 153).

Pauline resembles the women diagnosed with hysteria, whose bodies enact the repressed areas of bourgeois society. Since respectable women were required to distance themselves from lower bodily functions and indecent behavior, their only outlet for repressed behavior was in their apparently uncontrollable attacks of hysteria. Freud concluded that these attacks are "nothing but phantasies projected and translated into motor activity and represented in pantomime," though in a distorted form as a result of censorship (Freud, quoted in Stallybrass and White 1986: 174). In Freud's *Studies on Hysteria*, Frau Emmy von N. becomes frightened by the pictures in an ethnological atlas of American Indians dressed as animals in much the same way as Pauline is appalled by Fleur's transformation into a bear, because this affinity with animals is a threat to the "civilized" anti-instinctual bourgeois order. According to Julia Kristeva, the abject is the object or other that is constituted through primal repression and thus confronts us with those "fragile states where man strays on the territories of animal"[2] (Kristeva 1982: 12). Late nineteenth-century Europe compensated for its rejection of the carnival tradition by a "plundering of ethnographic material—masks, rituals, symbols—from colonized cultures" and an enactment of socially repressed behavior by victims of hysteria (Stallybrass and White 1986: 172).

The demonization and the exclusion of the carnivalesque has to be related to the victorious emergence of specifically bourgeois practices. . . . In one way or another Freud's patients can be seen as enacting desperate ritual fragments salvaged from a festive tradition. (Stallybrass and White 176)

However, Pauline is more successful at enacting masochistic than erotic behavior. She longs for the pleasures she senses between Fleur and Eli and begins to desire him, admiring his strong chest and hips. Because Eli is not attracted to her, Pauline uses love medicine to bewitch him into having sex with Sophie, entering Sophie's consciousness to make her seduce Eli. Eventually, Pauline's sexual frustration leads her to have an affair with Napoleon Morrissey and become pregnant. When Pauline discovers she is pregnant, she blames Satan as the "one who had pinned me with his horns" (Erdrich 1989: 133). She is determined to end the pregnancy but prevented from doing so by Bernadette Morrissey, Napoleon's sister. Pauline feels that the illegitimate birth would make her an outcast and that the fetus can avoid the "taint" of original sin only by avoiding birth.

When Pauline is forced to deliver the baby by Bernadette, she immediately rejects the child because it was "already fallen, a dark thing" (Erdrich 136). The spoons that Bernadette uses to pull the baby out left indentations on her temples which Pauline interprets as "marked by the devil's thumbs." Pauline considers her child dark both because of her dark skin and because she was conceived through sexual sin, which are comingled in Pauline's mind. For Pauline, the personal pain and guilt associated with this pregnancy are combined with the guilt of internalized colonization and the guilt she feels for Fleur's rape and for murdering the rapists when she helped Russell bar the door to the freezer. When Pauline mentally reenacts how she and her young cousin, Russell, barred the door to the meat locker, trapping the men inside, she imagines that she is the one to lower the bar and therefore the one that will be punished at the Judgment.

Pauline is as jealous of the maternal love between Fleur and her daughter as she is of the love between Fleur and Eli. She notices that all of Fleur's attention not given to Eli is bestowed on their daughter, Lulu, who is allowed to chatter and is dressed in pretty moccasins and beads. It seems as if Pauline really yearns for love from Fleur, the sensual love that Fleur gives Eli and Lulu. As she watches Fleur hold Lulu, she feels jealousy. Even when she first worked with Fleur in Argus, Pauline wanted to be near her, remembering what it was to again have female companions like the mother and sisters who died in the epidemic. When Pauline's odor becomes intolerable, Fleur finally gives her a bath with Lulu's help and Pauline finds herself enjoying the forbidden pleasure of being touched.

When Fleur and Lulu finally force Pauline to have a bath, the effort induces premature labor in Fleur, causing her to lose the baby and to almost lose Lulu, who runs out in the bad weather to bring help. Once again, as during Fleur's rape, Pauline proves as useless in saving lives as she is useful in ending them. Though Pauline feels guilt for yet another failure to help Fleur, her guilt is comingled with her desire to bring the "unsaved" child to Christ through death.

Despite her natural enjoyment of the bath's sensual pleasure, Pauline tries to resist it because she has renounced life and pleasure. She had begun starving herself even before she discovered her pregnancy, so Pauline didn't know how long she had been pregnant. She shows a tendency to pervert her instinctual desires and the pleasure of the maternal body into a death wish. "If language, like culture . . . concatenates an order, it does so precisely by repressing maternal authority and the corporeal mapping that abuts against it" (Kristeva 72). After giving birth and entering the convent, Pauline begins wearing underwear made from potato sacks that chafe her body and wearing her shoes on the wrong feet in the belief that her suffering allows her to identify with Christ's suffering. Pauline tries to deny her body any pleasure, not only sexual but even that of relieving her bladder. When Nanapush gives her tea and then teases her with a story about flooding in order to stimulate her need to urinate, she tries to resist temptation by thinking of Christ's love for martyrs.

Julia Kristeva, in *Powers of Horror*, explains the connection between sin and holiness. "The knowledge that would separate him from his natural, animal, and mortal state, enabling him to reach, through thought, purity and freedom, is fundamentally sexual knowledge. . . . That is so true that only after having sinned does the mystic topple over into holiness, and his holiness never ceases to appear to him as fringed by sin" (Kristeva 1982: 126). Kristeva interprets the evangelist Paul's message as a battle between the spirit and the overwhelming drives of the flesh. The outcome can only be death since a "subdued body" is a spiritual body (Kristeva 124). Thus sin and holiness, pleasure and pain are inseparable because subduing the body's drives provides the mystic with an "infinite *jouissance*, or a physical pleasure bordering on the sensual" (Mazzoni 1991: 65).

Pauline's subsequent rejection of sexuality is as extreme as her previous expression of it, the pain of abrasive clothing, hunger and uncomfortable shoes become as sensual as the sexual pleasure. Angela of Foligno abased herself by serving lepers and drinking the water with which she washed their sores. Pauline abases herself by enduring her various forms of self-mortification and by ministering to the Indians whom she considers abject and unholy. Especially after her brief sexual encounter that results in pregnancy, Pauline decides that Anishinaabeg culture as well as sexuality are pagan and evil. For her, being white and Catholic is the only protection from the evil of nature and natural instincts. This choice is also motivated by her belief that she must become white to survive because the old culture is being eradicated. Pauline combines her experience of personal and cultural loss with Catholicism's emphasis on suffering as an imitation of Christ and a means to personal salvation. While Fleur becomes obsessed with saving her children from death, and, on a larger scale, saving her people from losing their land and culture, Pauline reconciles herself to personal and cultural loss by embracing death as the path to salvation for herself and her people, whom she can offer to Christ once she delivers them into death from influenza and consumption. Pauline imagines that she tells Christ how many souls she has brought him and he asks her to bring more.

Pauline's preoccupation with death and becoming white are essentially the same. In order to become white, the nonwhite part of Pauline must die. Thus her masochistic self-destructive behavior is in reality related to her obsession with self-purification, which is distorted into a repression of her body, whose abject boundaries signify the threatened boundaries of the white or Christian order and the Anishinaabeg culture, both of which are endangered when confronted by alternative systems of meaning.[3] For Pauline becoming Catholic is equivalent to becoming white; racial purity signifies spiritual purity. In *Black Skin, White Masks*, Frantz Fanon explores the self-hatred among the colonized that results from their adoption of the European belief in white racial superiority: "The magazines are put together by white men for little white men . . . these same magazines are devoured by the local children. In the magazines the Wolf, the Devil, the Evil spirit, the Bad Man, the Savage are always symbolized by Negroes or Indians" (Fanon 1982: 146).

After giving birth, Pauline joins the convent and intensifies her bodily mortification to purge herself of personal and collective guilt. Denying herself sleep and food results in strange visions that tell her she is forgiven for her daughter and most importantly in which Christ tells her that she is not Indian but "wholly white" (Erdrich 1989: 137). This vision conveniently occurs just when the nuns received a directive not to admit "Indian girls." For Pauline, being white is essential as a survival strategy in a world that has become increasingly dominated by whites. She believes that God must have made the whites shrewder because they are successful while the Indians are clearly not protected by Misshepeshu because they are dying all around her. Of course, Pauline fails to recognize the role that the colonization process played in this cultural breakdown, especially the allotment system of the Dawes Act.[4] Pauline's ignorance of social and economic factors involved in the decline of her people combined with her self-hatred lead her to believe rather simplistically that this decline is a sign of God's disapproval of their dark skin and "pagan" beliefs.

Later when Nanapush is boiling herbs for Fleur's cure, Pauline plunges her hands into the boiling water, expecting them to be protected by Christ's power. When they are scalded, she interprets this as an indication that Christ is still weak in this country of devils and she decides to exorcise one of these devils, Misshepeshu, by going to the lake, engaging in battle with what she believes to be the water monster and eventually destroying it. Pauline had described the water monster as handsome and interested in pretty young women like Fleur, not in unattractive women like herself, a variation on her desire for Eli who also prefers Fleur. When she discovers that she has in reality killed her lover and the father of her child, Pauline decides that the devil had assumed the body of Napoleon.

If indeed, as Pauline suspects, she is kin to the Morrissey family, then she and this family, as well as Fleur, may have a special relationship to Misshepeshu. The name Morrissey is an Anglicized version of the Irish name Muirgheasa, derived from *muir* meaning sea and *geas* or *geis* meaning prohibition or obligation (Hanks and Hodges 1988: 376). In *No Country for Young Men*, the geis signifies irresistible and dangerous sexual attraction. The character Gráinne is named for the legendary Gráinne, who put a geis on Diarmuid forcing him to run away with her and endanger his life by angering her husband. "Pollution fears do not seem to cluster round contradictions which do not involve sex. The answer may be that no other social pressures are potentially so explosive as those which constrain sexual relations" (Douglas 1989: 157). The Gráinne story suggests that sexuality, like death, is dangerous. A taboo is generally associated with danger to the social order such as "the dead, [who] if not separated from the living bring madness on them" (Douglas 176). Indeed, Pauline, Nanapush and Fleur are all associated with powerful libidinal energy as well as proximity to the world of the dead in their prolonged mourning process.

In traditional cultures, the shaman mediates these dangerous realms and assists people emotionally and spiritually so that they are not isolated in dealing with emotional and physical illness and death and so that they can experience healing by transcending ordinary consciousness. Pauline's story resembles the story of Cora Sheppo, reported by Gerald Vizenor to illustrate the consequences when colonialism has eliminated the culturally supportive role of altered states such as shamanism. Like Pauline in *Tracks*, Cora "has bizarre delusions and thoughts of being controlled by external forces of the devil" (Vizenor 1984: 147). Pauline and Cora vacillate between Christianity and tribal religion. Pauline believes she is being attacked by the devil and that her illegitimate child is a "dark thing" because of sin. Cora believed she confronted evil forces and told the psychiatrist that she had experienced a feeling of death. Pauline tried to abort her child and even prevent its delivery. Cora tragically does succeed in killing her grandson who she believes was "spawned by the devil." According to Vizenor, "Cora Sheppo needed a shaman to rescue her soul and save her grandchild," because the shaman, as a healer, is "someone capable of ecstatic travel in search of lost souls" (Vizenor 148).

The emotional supports and the modes of collective solutions of the basic problems of existence available to the shaman . . . greatly alleviate the strain of an otherwise excruciatingly painful existence. Such supports are all too often completely unavailable to the schizophrenic in our culture. (Vizenor 148)

Vizenor relates the tendency toward pathologizing marginal people to that of categorizing native people as victims and suggests that these damaging representations do not reflect reality or show compassion for real people who survive through trickster strategies: "No sorcerer could survive the insipid tabulations. Meanwhile, there are tribal people in cities and on reservations who must resist data colonization, social science categorization, and shovel out the academic dossier to free their dreams and families" (Vizenor 28). When Nanapush decides to become a bureaucrat himself in order to retrieve Lulu from boarding school, he expresses a similar criticism, that his people are becoming a "tribe of file cabinets and triplicates, a tribe of single-space documents, directives, policy" (Erdrich 1989: 225).

Both Fleur and Pauline attempt to save their people single-handedly. They overestimate their power and then punish themselves for their failure. Nanapush tries to explain to Fleur that she is not to blame for the loss of tribal land or the death of her premature baby. Pauline's obsession with evil and guilt represent her splitting of good and evil into separate categories and her desire to split her Indian self from her white self. Yet Fleur also seems to hope for the impossible, a restoration of traditional land and culture from economic exploitation. Only Nanapush can accept the mixture of good and evil in human nature, the inability to prevent appropriation of Anishinaabeg land by whites and the postcolonization mixture of cultures as well as bloodlines. Nanapush however refuses to be broken by this process. He seems to realize that while overt resistance would fail, covert resistance can continue by passing on stories of survival and subversion.

Nanapush as trickster is a spokesperson for the frailty of human nature and the fragility of culture. "Trickster functions not so much to call cultural categories into question as to demonstrate the artificiality of culture itself" (Wiget 1985: 94). If Pauline represents the Christian method of self-sacrifice for the salvation of humanity, Nanapush represents an alliance between the traditional cultural trickster figure, who signifies the complexity of human nature capable of heroism and destructiveness, with the Christian model of compassion and humility. The priest, Father Damien, who befriends Nanapush and tries to help the Anishinaabeg understand government policies, indicates a compassionate alternative to Pauline's distorted form of Catholicism. When Eli comes to Nanapush expecting sympathy because Fleur has banished him after his escapades with Sophie, Nanapush berates Eli for his self-pity and tries to make him realize the importance of the tribal land issue and that, by comparison to what is happening to the tribe, Eli's problems are minor.

Similarly, Nanapush makes fun of Margaret when she is possessive of her son, Eli, and preoccupied with his love affair with Fleur. He implies that Margaret spies on Eli and Fleur because she is sexually frustrated. When she comments about the lake man, "I'll give him good as I get," Nanapush asks her, "Has it been that long, Margaret?" (Erdrich 1989: 50). While Nanapush often humorously criticizes human weaknesses, he is more tolerant of this weakness than the other characters are and is more forgiving of Pauline and Fleur than they are of themselves. He also acknowledges his weakness in realizing that he declines emotionally and physically when Margaret leaves him after a minor disagreement and recovers only when she returns to him.

Yet Nanapush is not merely the old fool he often claims to be. Even his statement that "I'm an old man far past anything a woman can do to weaken me" is contrary to the truth in trickster fashion, as later exemplified by his love affair with Margaret. Despite his age, he is able to heal both Fleur and later Lulu, bringing them back from the edge of death. He also instructs Eli in the lovemaking skills that he needs to win Fleur and guides him on the hunt, calling for his helpers until the "rattle started, the song sang itself" and he sees a vision of Eli's tracks (Erdrich 101).

Nanapush is acutely aware of the colonization that causes his people to lose their land because few of them could read the papers they signed. He is knowledgeable about the allotment system's effect on the tribe and understands how his people's trouble is caused by the money and liquor that has corrupted them so they don't notice that their land is being stolen from them. Nanapush, however, resists the pressure to sell and also refuses to give his real name to the government bureaucrats because he knows it "loses power every time that it is written and stored in a government file" (Erdrich 32). Nanapush understands how the breakdown of community and culture resulting from colonization, combined with the desire to survive and the temptation of greed, can damage people so much that they betray one another.

Yet despite his trickster skills in healing, hunting, lovemaking, storytelling and political subversion, Nanapush remains humble, forgiving his and others failings and never taking his power for granted. Nanapush admits his human frailty and his need to depend on the supernatural despite the fact that it is unpredictable and failed to protect his people from devastation. Thus though transgressive and powerful, Nanapush is a compassionate tribal trickster who recognizes the unreliability of power: "As soon as you rely on the possession it is gone. Forget that it ever existed, and it returns" (Erdrich 177).

Nanapush's trickster skills exemplify Vizenor's emphasis on a mythic and ecstatic oral tradition that evokes a complex and fluid reality not captured by academic abstractions about the Anishinaabeg. The mythic or shamanic perspective expressed in *Tracks* permits fluid boundaries between animal and human, life and death. People can become bears and souls can be retrieved from the world of the dead. Human and animal hierarchies don't exist. In the Anishinaabeg worldview, humans exist within nature not above it. The fluidity of this worldview is related to the necessity of reciprocity among people and between people and animals for survival: "Great stress [is] laid upon sharing what one has with others. . . . Hoarding, or any manifestation of greed, is discountenanced" (Hallowell 1975: 172). Similarly, one must not offend the animals upon which one depends for food: "It may be necessary, for example, to throw their bones in the water or to perform a ritual in the case of bears. Otherwise, he will offend the masters and be threatened with starvation because no animals will be made available to him" (Hallowell 172). Other traditional values include not overestimating one's power, not being greedy and having humility and respect, especially regarding nonhuman persons. These Anishinaabeg values of sharing with others or respecting the natural resources are antithetical to capitalism, which encourages the individual accumulation of wealth.

Erdrich validates the oral traditions of Anishinaabeg culture through the character of Nanapush. Some of what we know about Fleur and the other characters is outside the novel either because it occurs in Erdrich's other novels about these characters, such as Fleur's reappearance in *The Bingo Palace*, or it is based on oral stories that are alluded to but not actually recorded in the novel, such as the stories Nanapush tells Fleur, Eli and Lulu. When Fleur and Nanapush are windigo because they are filled with the souls of their dead, Father Damien's arrival causes Nanapush to begin speaking to convince himself that he is alive. "I talked both languages in streams that ran alongside each other, over every rock, around every obstacle" (Erdrich 1989: 7). Later in the novel when Lulu's feet are frozen and Nanapush heals her with stories, there is a similar scene alluding to these stories that aren't contained in the novel's text but that have the maternal power to bring Lulu back to life. "Once I had you I did not dare break the string between us and kept on moving my lips, holding you motionless with talking. . . . I talked on and on until you lost yourself inside the flow of it . . . [and] were sustained" (Erdrich 167).

The woodland creation stories are told from visual memories and ecstatic strategies, not from scriptures. In the oral tradition, the mythic origins of tribal people are creative expressions, original eruptions in time, not a mere recitation or a recorded narrative in grammatical time. (Vizenor 1984: 7)

Some readers, such as Gloria Bird, have wondered about Fleur's silence, interpreting it as a result of colonialism. "In the novel, hers is the only consciousness that remains inaccessible to us as readers. Our knowledge of her is shaped solely through second-hand means analogous to the way in which the construct of savagism has been informed" (Bird 1992: 45). While I agree that her apparent silence is related to the impact of colonialism, Fleur is silent only in a colonialist interpretation of voice.

Given the need for secrecy by subversives such as Fleur's grandson Gerry, who is an American Indian Movement (AIM) activist in *Love Medicine*, Fleur's apparent silence protects her from misrepresentation or betrayal. On two occasions in the novel, Fleur "speaks" eloquently with her actions. The first time is when she renegotiates the terms of her rape by shedding doubt on the paternity of Lulu. She does this by engaging in overt public sexual activity with Eli in the woods. The second time is when she resists the lumber company by enacting the deforestation of her land before they can do so. She sawed each tree through at the base so that the now entirely illusory forest fell to the ground with one stroke. Fleur leaves different tracks than the conventional print version, just as her footprints appear to transform into bear tracks in the novel. Her voice is heard in oral tradition beyond the textual realm like Nanapush's stories that aren't heard by the reader.[5] *Tracks* could represents her text since the word "tracks" is used both for her bear tracks and for the printed word. Erdrich's later novel, *The Bingo Palace* ends with Fleur entering the world of the dead once more and leaving her tracks behind her.

She didn't take the written walls, she didn't take the storehouse facts. She didn't take the tangled scribe of her table or the headboard, the walls, the obscured and veiny writing on the tamped logs and her bed. . . . No, all of the writing, the tracked-up old cabin, she left for the rest of us to find. (Erdrich, 1995: 272)

Pauline and Nanapush are tricksters who imagine the world, including the legendary Fleur, who is narrated through their dual perspectives. Meanwhile, Fleur is the trickster hidden on the margins of the text, like the oral traditions that can't be translated into print, and she is leaving tracks that are interpreted by Nanapush and Pauline from their respective worldviews while remaining hidden behind their narratives. Of the three characters, Pauline functions most like the traditional trickster,

Naanabozho, because she is the one who instructs by contraries, suffering the consequences of disobeying the traditional ethos. Nanapush, on the other hand, is ironically the character who most embodies the traditional Anishinaabeg ethos, with his emphasis on generosity, reciprocity and humility and especially on not overestimating one's power.

Pauline, Fleur and Nanapush are tricksters not by choice but by having been thrust into this position by their experience of death and cultural conflict. At the end of *Tracks*, Nanapush explains to Lulu that he is telling her all these stories of the past, especially about her mother, Fleur, so that she will understand that Fleur didn't send her to boarding school to punish her but to protect her, because historical events have ensured that there would be no safety for Lulu on the reservation as long as it is dominated by the United States government and exploited by companies like the Turcot Lumber Company.

Vizenor recounts several stories of Naanabozho, the variations illustrating the imaginative artistry of tellers. Nanapush's mother is a maiden who was impregnated by a *manidoo* (variant spelling of *manito*). She dies or is abducted by the *manidoo* and Nanapush is raised by her mother, his grandmother. Nanapush gambles against the great gambler, "a person who seemed almost round in shape, smooth and white," for the souls of his people (Vizenor 1984: 5). Louise Erdrich "relumes" the Nanapush story in *Tracks*. Fleur is impregnated with Lulu either by Misshepeshu, the water man, or by Eli, her lover, or by the white men who rape her after she defeats them at cards. Fleur saves Lulu's life by gambling with the ghosts of her dead white rapists. Thus Erdrich retells the Nanapush story, adapting it to postcolonial culture, providing a stronger role for the female character and confounding the identity of Naanabozho/Nanapush.

NOTES

1. Nanapush uses the term "Anishinaabe" for his people whereas Pauline uses Chippewa. I will use Anishinaabeg except when quoting from sources that use Chippewa. According to Vizenor, "In the language of the tribal past, the families of the woodland spoke of themselves as the Anishinaabeg (plural of Anishinaabe) until the colonists named them the Ojibway and Chippewa. . . . Tribal people used the word Anishinaabeg to refer to the people of the woodland who spoke the same language. The collective name was not an abstract concept of personal identities or national ideologies. Tribal families were the basic political and economic units in the woodland and the first source of personal identities" (Vizenor 1984: 13).

2. Since the abject is a fragile and "archaic . . . sublimation of an 'object,' " it evokes the threat of falling back into the pre-symbolic realm of animals or of absorption by the maternal entity (Kristeva 1982: 12).

3. "The danger of filth represents for the subject the risk to which the very symbolic order is permanently exposed, to the extent that it is a device of discriminations, of differences. But from where and from what does the threat issue? From nothing else but . . . the frailty of the symbolic order itself" (Kristeva 69).

4. See D. S. Otis, *The Dawes Act and the Allotment of Indian Lands.* According to Otis, since the designers of the Dawes Act believed that the "white man's way was good and the Indian's way was bad . . . allotment was counted on to break up tribal life" and foster individually owned farms (Otis 1973: 9).

5. The relationship between oral tradition and the "orality" of *Tracks* has been examined by Joni Clarke in "Why Bears Are Good to Think and Theory Doesn't Have to be Murder: Transformation and Oral Tradition in Louise Erdrich's *Tracks.*" Joni's article suggested to me the possibility that there is an orality that exceeds the text just as the sexuality of the characters exceeds the text and this orality is implied only through its residue or "tracks" on the margins of the novel.

3
~ *Myal* ~

By voicelessness, we mean the historical absence of the woman writer's text: the absence of a specifically female position on major issues. . . . By voicelessness we also mean silence: the inability to express a position in the language of the "master" as well as the textual construction of woman as silent.

Davies and Fido 1990: 1

Like Fleur, in *Tracks,* who publicly enacts passionate sexuality, Ella O'Grady of Erna Brodber's novel *Myal* "speaks" when her body discharges waste that produces a violent storm during her healing by Mass Cyrus. Her healing transforms Ella from a zombie, "rigid, staring, silent" into a force of nature, a tempest. She is racially mixed like Pauline and has suffered similar, though less extreme, confusion about her racial identity. Ella has become ill through being psychosexually dispossessed of herself due both to her colonial upbringing and her American husband, Selwyn, both of which split "whiteness" and "blackness" into binary opposites. Her response to this dispossession is not expressed in the master's language but rather through her body's mimicry of pregnancy and her repetition of the cryptic phrase, "Mammy Mary's mulatto mule must have maternity wear" (Brodber 1988: 84).

Mass Cyrus diagnoses Ella as "choked on foreign, this alabaster baby" (Brodber 4). He interprets her illness as a condition of being racially and culturally in-between and recognizes that she can be cured only by allowing the woods and trees in his grove to heal her. Because Mass Cyrus worries that Ella will harm his grove with the "bam-bam" when she releases "that gray mass of muck," he removes her from his grove before the healing is finished. When

Ella releases the waste that bloated her belly, the impact of this event destroys "71,488 coconut trees, 3,470 breadfruit trees, 901 residences totally, 203 residences partially, 628 out-buildings, and left 65 standing but damaged . . . several humans lost their lives from drowning in the thunder storm and swollen rivers that it brought" (Brodber 4). As he observes the damage to the environment, Mass Cyrus asks, "What nigger for to do?" which is a line from a slave song about resistance and the fight for freedom.

> Buckra in this country no make we free
> What Negro for to do? What Negro for to do?
> Take force by force! Take force by force. (cited by Brathwaite 1971: 211)

The destructive storm that results when Ella discharges her colonial waste is a motif that suggests Shakespeare's *The Tempest* and Césaire's *Une Tempête*, with their Prospero/Caliban dyads of colonizer/colonized. Mass Cyrus refers to the results of Ella's healing as a lightening storm and a thunder storm, not as a tempest or a hurricane. According to Peter Hulme, the word "tempest" is preferred in Shakespeare because a tempest is "interpretable through the master code of Providence," while the Arawak derived word "hurricane" is "less a message from god for his chosen people than an aspect of savagery" (Hulme 1986: 99,102,). Ella's storm is a revision of these meanings because it is neither a sign from a Christian god nor a sign of savagery but a consequence of the destructive effects of colonialism. The year of this event is 1919, a year that saw the development of strikes and a labor movement in Jamaica and the rising influence of Jamaica-born Marcus Garvey's pan-African movement. Joyce Walker-Johnson examines the context of *Myal* and its 1919 setting in particular, a year of rioting and civil disturbances that signified a new phase of resistance among Jamaicans, a turning point in the condition of formerly enslaved and still colonized people.

The freak storm in his grove may be understood as a reference to the reverberations from the disturbances in 1919. He [Mass Cyrus] anticipates a chain reaction when the "gray mass" (a metonymic rendering of "brain" and hence, "ideas") starts oozing out of the "rigid, staring, silent female." (Walker-Johnson 1992: 55)

Through various clues in the novel, Brodber represents Ella's healing process as an evolution of the colonized consciousness from a state of voiceless zombification to self-awareness and self-expression through political acts and ideological resistance to colonialism. Thus slave rebellions are linked to the postslavery labor movement and slave songs of resistance are related to Bob

Marley's reggae songs with their anticolonial message. Brodber asserts this
continuity by having Mass Cyrus say "What nigger for to do?" from a slave
song and Ole African with his "dreadful hair" repeatedly say "The half has
never been told" from "Get Up, Stand Up," a Bob Marley song that states:
"Half the history has never been told [a]nd now that the children have seen the
light [t]hey're gonna stand up for their right" (Waters 1985: 1). These songs
belong to oral traditions that keep alive the stories of resistance that haven't
been recorded in the printed histories.

The subjugation of Africans by force was accompanied by the attempt to instill in
them, both physically and culturally a sense of their own inherent
inferiority . . . [yet] Africans have resisted both slavery and colonialism; indeed
even before they left the continent itself. (Chevannes 1994: 10)

In Jamaica, this resistance has taken the form of slave rebellions, the
postslavery Morant Bay Rebellion of 1865, the 1919 strike wave and the
general strike of 1938. It has also been expressed in the revivals of indigenous spirituality such as Myal and the Rastafari movement and in the continued subversive use of oral tradition from slave songs to reggae. The
traditional African culture that was denigrated as vulgar or inferior by the
colonizer is being reclaimed by Jamaican authors and musicians such as
Erna Brodber and Bob Marley.

The casual centrality of the "supernatural" in Brodber's fiction is also an excellent
example of the writer's adaptation of marginalised thematic concepts from the oral
tradition. . . . What Brodber actually writes in *Myal* is an alternative curriculum
that challenges the process of zombification whereby the colonized/educated mind
assumes the convenient state of living dead, easily manipulable. (Cooper 1993: 3)

Brodber's first novel, *Jane and Louisa Will Soon Come Home*, was intended as a study in abnormal psychology. While Frantz Fanon provided
insight into the psychology of black colonized males, Brodber presents insight into the psychologically damaged Jamaican woman through the character of Nellie, who eventually learns self-love with help from Baba, an
"anancy [trickster]" (Brodber 1980: 69). Nellie, like Ella in *Myal*, "travels to
'foreign' to study and returns home to a profound sense of homelessness
from which she is redeemed only when she comes to understand the oral
accounts of her fragmented family history and the distorted perceptions of
female identity and sexuality that she has internalized in childhood" (Cooper 1990: 280). *Louisiana* is the title and the assumed name of the central
character, Ella Townsend, in Brodber's third novel. Ella is an anthropologist who adopts native customs and abandons her stance of detached ob-

server while collecting oral history of the blacks of southwest Louisiana. The book claims to be posthumously based on Ella's manuscript, an account of how her fieldwork evolved into her role as a psychic whose communication with her deceased informant resulted in the recovery of people's histories, including her family history.

The character of Ella O'Grady in Brodber's second novel, *Myal*, has some qualities in common with Ella Townsend/Louisiana and Nellie because she is educated in "foreign" yet interested in recovering lost history and culture. As a light-skinned, racially mixed Jamaican woman with a Jamaican mother and an Irish father, Ella O'Grady is the embodiment of Jamaica's complex history of slavery and racism and her body rebels against this history. The use of physical force to maintain the institution of slavery was buttressed by ideological arguments for the inferiority of African peoples: "The Europeans evolved a sophisticated and carefully calibrated hierarchy of skin tones, beginning with themselves at the very top and descending to pure African at the very base" (Chevannes 1994: 9). Even in recent years, the darkest Jamaicans are at the lowest rung of the socioeconomic hierarchy. Though Ella's light-skin privilege is resented by her darker classmates, she is not light enough for her white husband, who tries to make her all white.

"A second line of attack was against the culture of the Africans. Strenuous efforts were made, if not to cause the people to forget Africa, at least to make them think of it as an uncivilized, primitive place" (Chevannes 10). The colonization process by which she has become the "living dead" is revealed in the novel. Ella's colonial education teaches her the superiority of European culture and the inferiority of her African ancestry. Ella's violent healing catharsis is followed by a flashback to Ella at age thirteen reciting Kipling's poem about the "whiteman's burden," which describes black people as "[h]alf devil and half child" (Brodber 1988: 6). This poem's binary relationship between black and white demonstrates the basis for the split identity of a racially mixed person like Ella.

She is also in-between because her typical colonial education describes English culture and even English landscapes inhabited by light-skinned people, while she lives in the "country bush of yam vines, coco roots and coconut trees" inhabited by dark-skinned people (Brodber 6). Colonial texts inform Ella that black people are "half-devils" and Calibans, who need to be civilized by the white colonizer, yet she must enact this conflict internally since she is both black and white.

Ella has been ostracized by her classmates because they think that she is too white. Only in colonial texts does Ella encounter light-skinned people like her. "She met Peter Pan and she met the Dairy Maid who could pass for her sister -same two long plaits and brownish" (Brodber 11). Through reading these stories, Ella travels in her imagination to other worlds: "She had been to England several times. To Scotland too and had watched them playing the bagpipes. . . . Peter had taken her into a coal mine and up through a chimney and she had come out looking more like her mother" (Brodber 11). Eventually the Reverend Brassington's white wife notices Ella and feels concern for her in-between condition. Maydene Brassington has observed and understood her husband's difficult position of being racially mixed and is concerned that he has adapted himself to the colonizing culture. When Maydene listens to Ella's recitation of Kipling, she recognizes a parallel to William.

He must have grown up like that little girl. One strange face in a sea of colour. Lonely among his own people. . . . That little girl looked as if she was flying.[1] Totally separated from the platform and from the people around her. (Brodber 17)

Maydene realizes that Ella is not happy with her ethereal existence in the sky, her soul split from her body, and that "[s]he wants to be real" (Brodber 17). She understands this as the process of spirit thievery that the white colonizer and missionary have enacted on the native people by separating them from their culture and spirituality. Because her husband insists that the people in his congregation wear European-style clothes and abandon their headdresses and colorful attire, Maydene complains to William that he is "taking away these people's spirit" (Brodber 18). Realizing that this is the result of William's fear of his non-European ancestry, Maydene adopts Ella at least in part to help William. Given the nature of colonial education, which polarizes white and black, racially mixed people like William and Ella are put in the schizoid position of believing they must be either one race or the other. Consequently, William and Ella have repressed their connection to African culture. Because Maydene would like to help William by helping Ella reconnect her soul to her body and accept herself as a mixture of black and white, she asks Ella's mother for permission to take Ella into her home. Eventually, Maydene and William send Ella to Baltimore with Mrs. Johnny Burns and there she meets her husband, Selwyn Langley. He is introduced in the novel in a manner that suggests *Jane Eyre*'s Rochester, a man who had already used several mistresses to serve his needs and who eventually regarded his creole wife Bertha as contaminated due to her "prodigious" sexual desires.

If Selwyn Langley had been born in eighteenth or nineteenth century Britain and of upper class parentage. . . . he would have been sent off to Jamaica and would have met Ella O'Grady and chosen her from among his stock to be his housekeeper. He would have given her two children, made his fortune and returned to England. (Brodber 42)

Historically, poor Irish women were often servants of the English in other colonies as well as in Ireland. In *No Country for Young Men*, Michael comments on this traditional employment for the emigrant Irish woman with his description of their great-aunt, an elderly nun who comes to live with them: "Hers was the governess generation, Ireland had peopled the world with them" (O'Faolain 1980: 54). Ella's Jamaican mother was the housekeeper to the Irish policeman by whom she conceived Ella. Brodber's statement that if Selwyn Langley had been born in eighteenth- or nineteenth-century Britain he would have chosen Ella O'Grady to be his housekeeper suggests Lewis's remarks about white men who acquire brown women as mistresses "under the appellation of housekeepers." These women do much of the household labor as well as servicing the sexual appetites of their masters. "She is perpetually in the hospital, nurses the children, can bleed and mix up medicines. . . . This kind of connexion is considered by a brown girl in the same light as marriage" (Lewis 1845: 86–87).

Women servants like Ella's mother were often expected to become the master's mistress, and in this capacity, they were receptacles for the sexual needs and "waste" of colonial men. Alain Corbin's study of the function of "Commercial Sexuality in Nineteenth-Century France" connects the prostitute with that "chain of resigned female bodies, originating in the lower classes and bound to the instinctive physical needs of upper-class males," a chain that includes nursery maids and housekeepers, who like prostitutes are at the "beck and call of the bourgeois body" (Corbin 1986: 212–13). Thus prostitution is a method of segregating the dirt, or what is socially unacceptable, in order to preserve domestic order, just as colonialism can serve to segregate or exile the dirt of the metropole.

Selwyn and Rochester both attempt to transform their respective mates, Ella and Jane, through "spirit thievery." Jane Eyre is an orphan who becomes a governess to Rochester's daughter and eventually marries him after his "mad" wife Bertha burns to death. Rochester has constructed Bertha as animal and madwoman contrasted to Jane as "delicate and aerial" (Brontë 1971: 227). When he describes to Jane his intention of dressing her in satin, lace and jewels, Jane protests that he will make her into an "ape in a harlequin's jacket" (Brontë 228). Likewise Ella's suitor, Selwyn Langley, remakes Ella into a "full Irish girl" with the "powdering and the plucking of eyebrows, the straightening of the hair. . . . The creator loved his creature. . . . Just one teeny little lie; her parents had come from Ireland" (Brodber 1988: 43). As Spivak (1985) observes in "Three Women's Texts and a Critique of Imperialism," imperialism constructs the native, or creole in the case of Bertha, as savage, occupying the boundary between animal and human, in order to construct the colonizer as a European subject with a mission to civilize the native.

[Bertha] must play out her role, act out the transformation of her "self" into that fictive Other, set fire to the house and kill herself, so that Jane Eyre can become the feminist individualist heroine of British fiction. [We] must read this as an allegory of the general epistemic violence of imperialism, the construction of a self-immolating colonial subject. (Spivak 251)

Selwyn takes Ella's innocence when he explains to her that she is in fact not white but mulatto yet encourages her to pass as white/ Irish. Ella has already experienced the social alienation of being a light-skinned hybrid in the dark-skinned bush community. Now Selwyn, acting as anthropologist/colonizer, tries to civilize and whiten her thus alienating her even further from herself and her community. Ella has been both sexually and psychologically violated by her spouse and master, Selwyn Langley. The sexual violation occurs when Selwyn uses prophylactics without explaining this to Ella, who is too naive to understand why she doesn't become pregnant. She has been violated psychologically because Selwyn has stolen and rewritten her stories of her childhood in the bush: "He wanted to be in that room alone with her, to light a fire and have her take him into a tropical December and have her show him its jungle and tell him its strange tales" (Brodber 1988: 46).

Not only does Selwyn steal her stories like Prospero stole Caliban's knowledge of the island, but he also transforms them into a colonial text that is entirely different. Ella's mother and Ella are not represented in their shades of light or mixed skin color. Ella is a white-skinned girl with "flowing blonde hair" and the Grove Town characters are totally in black-face, like a minstrel show: "The black of their skins shone on stage, relieved only by the white of their eyes and the white of the chalk around their mouths. Everybody's hair was in plaits and stood on end and everybody's clothes were the strips of cloth she had told him Ole African wore" (Brodber 83). The last words Ella speaks while watching the play are "It didn't go so." The restoration of this colonial binary logic of black and white shocks Ella, who now realizes that her mulatto identity is outside of this binary system. This shock produces the psychosomatic pregnancy, which is really constipation with colonial waste. As Ella watches the play, she discovers the way it steals the spirit and voice of the colonized and constructs a racist duality of colonizer and colonized, civilized and savage, Prospero and Caliban, Jane and Bertha. Caliban, Bertha and the Grove Town people are constructed by the colonizer as the projected "dark thing" from within himself, the dark thing being his natural instincts, especially his sexuality.

Ella believes that because she is a mulatto, neither pure white nor pure black, she is bad or dirty. As the drain for colonial waste, she is bloated because her bowels are filled with feces. Selwyn has appropriated both Ella's biological reproductive capacity and her textual reproductive capacity or her stories. The trauma of this double appropriation is fully realized by Ella as she watches Selwyn's play, thus bringing her to the state of zombification described in the novel's opening scene. An unfortunate reminder of her own apparent sterility, Selwyn represents Grove Town as unnaturally fruitful.

There were breadfruits at the same time as there were star-apples as there were mangoes. . . . It was unnatural and it shook Ella but all her obsessed soul could register was: "Everything is a fruit except me." (Brodber 1988: 83)

After seeing the play and realizing the extent to which her innermost self has been appropriated and misrepresented, Ella stops speaking: "A couple months more and her belly was over-sized. She was carrying the baby Jesus. Then she stopped uttering completely. Stopped doing anything. Even stopped going to the lavatory" (Brodber 83). Ella believes that because she is "dirty," she cannot let Jesus enter "through the right door." She also thinks that Selwyn "has given fruit to everyone except me." The fruitfulness of Selwyn's play results from his translation of her stolen stories and reproductive capacity into the textual magic of his play. Selwyn's perversion of both her biological reproduction and of her cultural reproduction or stories has produced Ella's madness.

Evelyn O'Callaghan analyzes the motif of madness in novels by female Caribbean authors, including Erna Brodber's *Jane and Louisa Will Soon Come Home*. She especially concentrates on the character of Antoinette/Bertha in Rhys's *Wide Sargasso Sea*. Rhys's novel is a revision of Bertha's story from *Jane Eyre*, in which she is the mad wife that Rochester has locked in his attic. In Rhys's version, Rochester is responsible for Antoinette's madness because he has degraded her and stripped her of her identity by even renaming her. Finally, he takes her to England, removing her from her home and cultural context. As a result, "Antoinette finds herself divided between cultures, between emotions, between roles/false-selves, between places, even between life and death, until she becomes a 'zombie' her 'true self' withdrawn and her physical body like a 'marionette,' enacting empty actions" (O'Callaghan 1985: 103). O'Callaghan mainly uses the theories of British psychologist R. D. Laing, which concentrate on the conflict between a false self, or mask, enacted publicly in order to please others and the person's submerged real identity. The figure of the madwoman can be seen then as a metaphor for the damaged West Indian psyche, the result of dominant-submissive relationships modeled on the colonizer-colonized contract.

> These women writers are dealing with the West Indian "quest for identity"—using the psychic damage and distorted self-image of the individual as metaphors for a kind of pervasive "illness" to which our societies are prone as a result of the colonial encounter. The interior schisms dramatized in fiction may be interpreted as the symptoms of the dangerous lack of ontological security still prevalent in our region. (O'Callaghan 104)

The mental confusion and indeed the schizoid split between body and soul, black and white in the colonized psyche of Ella can be found in the representations of this psychologically colonized state of consciousness in the other three novels. In *No Country for Young Men*, Judith's confused mind is compared to a bog. Like Ella who felt there was something like "gauze in her head where she supposed her mind should be," Sister Judith felt as if she were "living behind a sheet of glass. A shroud. Some insulating chemical." (Brodber 1988: 80; O'Faolain 1980: 200). In Erdrich's novel *Tracks,* Pauline, who is a mixture of white and Native American, becomes a nun because she wants to be completely white so that she will not suffer as she believes the Indians are destined to suffer. She has a vision of Jesus Christ, evidently induced by her self-imposed starvation, in which he tells her that she is not Indian but "wholly white" and Pauline's Christianity takes the form of pathological self-abuse because she hates her native ancestry. Delia, the main character in *Delia's Song*, is a young Chicana who wonders if she is going mad after having suffered many losses. Her condition resembles a Mexican folk disease called *susto* which is the loss of soul or vital essence that occurs especially among those who feel obligated to meet impossible expectations.

As evidenced by the emergence from madness into a new consciousness for at least some of these women characters, particularly Ella, "madness" can constitute an opportunity for a rebirth of the true self. As Selwyn is stealing Ella's stories of her childhood in rural Grove Town in order to cre-

ate his manichean play, he assists her in re-membering the fragments of her
Grove Town background and her identity that were buried under the Peter
Pan illusions of her colonial education. His violation is ultimately benefi-
cial because it reconnects her mind with her body and her split-off
Afro-Caribbean identity. The draining brought clarity so that Ella could remember the people and landscape of Grove Town. However, Ella is able to
overcome the shock of her colonization process and reintegrate her repressed culture only after her treatment by Mass Cyrus expels the waste of
colonial texts which clogs her psyche as well as her stomach with binary
representations:

For years there had been something like gauze in her head where she supposed her
mind to be. It stretched flat across her head, separating one section of her mind
from the other—the top section. At the bottom were Mammy Mary and them
Grove Town people. (Brodber 80)

Orlando Patterson's analysis of slavery as a form of social death is relevant to Ella's condition of zombification through spirit thievery. According
to Patterson, whose study of slavery encompassed Greco-Roman slavery as
well as the European use of African slaves in the Americas, slavery entails a
form of "forced alienation, the loss of ties of birth in both ascending and
descending generations. It also has the important nuance of a loss of native
status, of deracination. . . . The slave was the ultimate human tool, as
imprintable and as disposable as the master wished" (Patterson 1982: 7).
The master usually gave the slave a new name, just as Rhys's Rochester re-
names Antoinette as Bertha, thus stripping her or him of their identity as
nonslave. The slave's body was often marked in a particular way to signify
the slave's status as property, such marks included tattooing, branding,
scars from whipping. Because the slave was alienated from an identity and a
community, she or he was defined as a "socially dead person," a "nonbeing" (Patterson 38).

As Orlando Patterson observes in his study of slavery as social death, a
similar form of social death occurs among all oppressed people, whether
victims of slavery, colonization or other conditions of oppression: "It is
truly remarkable how consistent are the attributes of the expression of generalized dishonor not only among all slaves but among all oppressed peoples" (Patterson 12). Frantz Fanon addresses the continuation of this sense
of nonbeing or nonidentity in the colonized black person. Though Fanon's
treatment of women (black and white) as objects of exchange that confirm
the relative power status of males erases women's subjectivity, his assertion
that "black identity is shaped by the oppressive sociopolitical structure of

colonial culture" was a breakthrough in recognizing the psychological effects of internalized racism (Bergner 1995: 76).

If there is an inferiority complex, it is the outcome of a double process:
  —primarily, economic;
  —subsequently, the internalization—or, better, the epidermalization—of this
  inferiority. (Fanon 1982: 11)

Because the black person is conditioned to feel that blackness is evil, inferior, subhuman and even invisible, she or he has only two choices, either to become white, a self-negation, or to remain inferior and invisible, negated by society.

Fanon criticizes black women's preference for white or light-skinned men in order to reproduce children that are whiter and therefore more privileged than themselves yet does not criticize black men for internalizing a "white European identity through intellect, acculturation, and class privilege" (Bergner 1995: 84). Thus the concept of lactification also applies to the ability of light-skinned people to rise socioeconomically by adopting European culture and the values of colonial education. The Rastafaris, who are an implicit presence in *Myal* suggested both by the line from a Bob Marley song and by the "dreadful hair" of "Ole African," oppose this process of "separation from the self [which] does not result in death, but in madness" by validating their roots in the history of precolonial Africa and adopting "as many elements of the traditional culture as they could" (Chevannes 1994: 28; Waters 1985: 10).

Ella is raised in the bush, where she is isolated because of her whiteness. Even the teachers treat her as invisible in the classroom. However, through "osmosis" Ella absorbs and identifies with characters in her colonial texts just as she had absorbed the oral traditions and natural phenomena of the bush. Her condition resembles the socially liminal condition of the slave or the colonized hybrid: "Once more unrecognized, Ella would stare through the windows. . . . When they brought out the maps and showed Europe, it rose from the paper in three dimensions, grew big, came right down to her seat and allowed her to walk on it" (Brodber 1988: 11).

In Patterson's and Fanon's descriptions of the social death or nonbeing of the colonized person, we recognize not only Ella's condition of zombification but also the similar conditions of characters in the other novels who are caught in a threshold state between being alive and being dead. Delia, in *Delia's Song*, repeatedly wonders if she is "already dead" and arrives at a Day of the Dead party so disheveled that she resembles "Dracula the undead." (Corpi 1989: 69) Pauline, in *Tracks*, is midwife to the dead and dying. She not only handles the dead, washing and dressing their bodies for burial, but she even assists the dying to enter into death. "Perhaps, hand over hand, I could have drawn her back to shore, but I saw very clearly that she wanted to be gone. . . . That is why I put my fingers in the air between us, and I cut where the rope was frayed down to string" (Erdrich 1989: 68).

In *No Country for Young Men*, some of the characters, especially Judith and Gráinne, seem to inhabit a liminal, threshold space. Gráinne's son, Cormac, refers to the women at the shelter they visit as zombies. Gráinne, in conversation with James, wonders if it's Halloween because the "souls of the dead seem to be about" and she feels as if she is "between worlds" (O'Faolain 1980: 96). There are frequent references in *No Country for Young Men* to the "slave mind" of the Irish and, in fact, there are historical precedents for associating the Irish with slavery (O'Faolain 72). In 1652 an Act of Settlement was decreed to evict the native population from land that was to compensate Cromwell's as yet unpaid soldiers, and this confiscation was justified as representing retribution for Protestant losses in the 1641 Irish Catholic rebellion against Protestant rule. "About two hundred of the most prominent leaders of the rising were actually executed; but thousands of young Irish men and women were shipped out as slaves to the sugar plantations in Barbados and to Jamaica, which had recently been conquered from Spain" (Costigan 1970: 81).

The figure of Caliban, from Shakespeare's *The Tempest* and Césaire's *Une Tempête*, is a presence that haunts *Myal* and could be based as much on English perceptions of the "savage" Irish as on knowledge of the "savage" Caribbean native. Shakespeare's *The Tempest* was first performed in 1611, fifteen years after Edmond Spenser wrote *A View of the Present State of Ireland*, which represents the Irish as barbarians and shows concern lest the colonizing English be corrupted by their proximity to such "strange and heathenish" customs: "Is it possible that an Englishman brought up naturally in such sweet civility as England affords could find such liking in that barbarous rudeness that he should forget his own nature and forgo his own nation?" (Spenser 1970: 48).

The colonial texts by Spenser and Shakespeare demonstrate an anxiety to preserve boundaries between Irish and English, Miranda and Caliban. *Myal*, in contrast, recognizes Ella O'Grady's mixed Irish and Afro-Caribbean descent as the outcome of British colonization of Ireland and Jamaica. Neither the culture itself or the subjectivities of the colonized can regain a precolonial purity. Jamaican writer Edward Brathwaite and others describe this process of creolization as the interaction of various cultures, indigenous, Afro-Caribbean and Euro-Caribbean, with the environment and with each other.[2] In Brodber's novel, boundaries between personal and political, colonizer and colonized, "madness" and sanity are explored, and a new postcolonial identity embraces the intersection of precolonial (African-Caribbean) and colonial symbolic systems. Colonialist discursive representations of the colonial encounter have tried to deny this dissolution of boundaries by establishing divisions between mind and body, savage and civilized, nature and society that disempower and disembody colonized men and women as well as their colonizers.

When colonial education forced Ella to be white, this made her abstract, a soul without a body, "[s]wimming in the sky, or flying or whatever, in that ethereal fashion over all below" (Brodber 1988: 17). Eventually, sexual relations with Selwyn begins to reconnect her disembodied mind with her material body. The construction of white European colonizer as disembodied mind and the colonized native as mindless body can be traced to texts such as Shakespeare's *The Tempest,* in which Prospero is the civilizing intellectual who describes Caliban as a "born devil, on whose nature Nurture can never stick" (Shakespeare 1987: 105). Thus this Caliban is as resistant to civilizing influences as wilderness might be resistant to cultivation.

As colonizer, Prospero and his successor Selwyn, the Prospero of Brodber's novel, steal the natives' knowledge and use it to destroy and exploit nature, transforming it into the waste of empire. According to Caliban, he gave Prospero his knowledge of the natural environment because "I loved thee and showed thee all the qualities o' th'isle, the fresh springs, brine-pits, barren place and fertile" (Shakespeare 45). Aime Césaire's Caliban, in *Une Tempête,* accuses Prospero of walking on the earth as a conqueror in contrast to his own respectful treatment of the earth:

You think the earth itself is dead. . . . It's so much simpler that way! Dead, you can walk on it, pollute it, you can tread upon it with the steps of a conqueror. I respect the earth, because I know that it is alive. (Césaire 1985: 15)

Like Césaire's Caliban, Brodber's Mass Cyrus communicates empathically with nature. He is surrounded by trees and shrubs and "[o]n their shoulders he always placed the sin-generated afflictions of the human world. They felt it" (Brodber 1988: 2). Thus Ella's reclamation of her body and its connection to the natural environment is related both to her identity as a colonized person and to the specifically sexualized form this takes in colonized females. It is essential to her cure that Ella is left there on the land to be healed by her contact with the animate landscape. The natural landscape in which her healing occurs vibrates because it is absorbing the pain and confusion of Ella and the discomfort of Mass Cyrus who is attempting to heal this pain. The landscape, as well as its human inhabitants, suffers the pain of colonization. Even Nellie, the caterpillar feels the "bitter vibrations" coming from Mass Cyrus:

Poor little thing. Inside her furry coat the thin strip of flesh that was her body, trembled so violently that her feet, many though they were, could not hold the ground but skated her across the earth. (Brodber 2)

Ella's body is the painful site in which the symbolic systems of colonizer and colonized conflict and mingle. Her Irish father as well as her Caribbean mother are both British colonial subjects and yet her father collaborates with colonialism as a policeman sent to maintain order. Caliban is portrayed as having a grotesque body because, as Peter Hulme has indicated in *Colonial Encounters*, "[t]he island is the meeting place of the play's topographical dualism . . . ground of the mutually incompatible reference systems whose co-presence serves to frustrate any attempt to locate the island on a map [and] Caliban is similarly the ground of these two discourses" (Hulme 1986: 108). He therefore exists both as more physical than Prospero, a native body contrasted to European mind, and as a discursive construct, his deformity signifying the intersection of incompatible symbolic systems.

Caliban, as an incarnation of a new category of the human, that of the subordinated "irrational" and "savage" native is now constituted as the lack of the "rational" Prospero, and the now capable-of-rationality-Miranda, by the Otherness of his/its physiognomic "monster" difference. (Wynter 1990: 358–59)

Prospero fears the monstrous reproduction that could occur between Miranda and Caliban through which the island would become peopled with Calibans. In Brodber's novel, this fearsome hybridity has already occurred. Ella's mulatto body is simply a sign of a more threatening hybridity—the mingling of symbolic orders until there is no clear cultural distinction between colonizer and colonized. Ella is also an anomaly constructed from the Calibans of Shakespeare and Césaire combined with the Jane Eyre-Bertha dyad of Charlotte Brontë and Jean Rhys. She has been zombified by her colonial education, and her body undergoes grotesque transformations due to its colonization by her American husband, Selwyn, who appropriates her knowledge.

The epistemic violence of imperialism is illustrated by the relationship of Prospero and Caliban. Prospero's secret studies in a fledgling, renaissance science enabled him to control the elements and to enslave Caliban, who is

vulnerable as a result of his charity toward Prospero. Untouched by the individualism of the emerging capitalist ethic, Caliban shared his knowledge
of nature on the island freely thus enabling Prospero to survive. Driven by
his Faustian will to power, Prospero appropriated this knowledge, as
Selwyn does with Ella's knowledge of Grove Town. He thereby usurped
Caliban's position as master of the island, defining Caliban as a bestial, subhuman creature, Spivak's "self-immolating colonial subject."

Prospero's magic is spirit thievery and manipulation of his environment.
Caliban and Prospero represent the encounter between precolonial ways of
knowing and the epistemological methods of renaissance science. The real
epistemic violence of colonization is the attempt to separate cultures and values into polarities of good and evil, savage and civilized, white magic and black
magic. Césaire's reinterpretation of the *The Tempest* explicitly portrays
Prospero's magic as the profane, new scientific method that professes heretical
theories about the shape of the earth and the possibility of discovering other
lands. Caliban counters Prospero's scientific method with his knowledge of
the natural world as a living ecosystem. Caliban accuses the imperialist
usurper Prospero of keeping his "science and know-how . . . for yourself
alone, shut up in big books," whereas the native Caliban generously "taught
you the trees, fruits, birds, the seasons" (Césaire 1985: 14).

Brodber expands on this critique by questioning the inherent violence of
certain types of knowledge. "The kind that splits the mind from the body
and both from the soul" (Brodber 1988:28). The story of Mass Levi and
Anita is a subtext in *Myal*. Mass Levi had been district constable and both
morally and physically strong. As he aged and became impotent, he engaged in spirit possession of Anita, an attractive, intelligent, fif-
teen-year-old, with the intention of recovering his sexual potency. When
Anita is kept awake by stones falling on the roof and a strange presence in
her bed, the community gathers to perform a healing and Mass Levi is discovered dead in the latrine with a doll resembling Anita.

Both Anita and Ella were exposed to knowledge and pedagogies that split
their minds from their bodies and "both from the soul and leaves each open
to infiltration" (Brodber 28). Thus the initial violation of their psyches by
an alienating form of knowledge left the women open to subsequent viola-
tions by men. Both women are healed through a form of Myalism, a religious movement that believed misfortunes such as poverty, illness and
oppression were caused by European sorcery and that emphasized possession by the Holy Spirit. "Its initiation ritual, which he called the 'myal
dance,' provided invulnerability to death caused by Europeans, that is European sorcery. According to Long, candidates enacted a ritual of death

and rebirth . . . dancing until they reached a state of dissociation resembling death" (Schuler 1979: 67).

Whereas Christianity placed its emphasis on transmitted knowledge. . . . Myal placed its emphasis on the experience of the Spirit. When followers found him it was to be filled by him, to be possessed. (Chevannes 1994: 19)

After Selwyn has drained her of the Grove Town stories, he begins to lose interest in her because he is preoccupied with writing his play based on her stories. Ella simultaneously begins to wonder why she isn't pregnant. Because of the prevalent racist belief in colonial Jamaica that miscegenation results in sterile or feeble offspring, Ella wonders if her mulatto condition has made her unable to reproduce. The term mulatto is derived from mule, the sterile offspring of a horse and a donkey. In his nineteenth-century *Journal of a Residence among the Negroes in the West Indies,* Matthew Lewis observed that, in fact, mulattoes were not sterile. "Since my arrival in Jamaica, I have reason to believe the contrary, and that mulattoes breed together just as well as blacks and whites; but they are almost universally weak and effeminate persons" (Lewis 1845: 55).

For sometime after viewing Selwyn's play, Ella doesn't speak. When she finally does, her only words are "Mammy Mary's mulatto mule must have maternity wear" (Brodber 1988: 84). "Mule" is an insulting reference to a barren woman in Jamaica. Ella's statement is a refusal to deny her hybrid origins, black mother and white father. Although Ella's voice is seldom heard in *Myal,* the reader sees the world from inside her mind and her painful struggles with dispossession. Ella has the advantage of being able to participate in both bush or British colonial symbolic systems since she is on the margins of both. While her anomalous body is still constructed through (the master's) language, it cannot be controlled by language. Ella's body, which has been invaded and drained psychosexually by her husband and then filled by his racist play with the refuse of imperialism, is able to release this waste with the aid of the Myal man, Mass Cyrus. Through the storm generated by her body, Ella manages to resist both definition by Selwyn and containment by the text.

Ella's illusory pregnancy refers to traditional Jamaican health beliefs regarding women and "gender-linked role expectations and ideas about the dangers of male-female relationships" (Sobo 1997: 145). Jamaican men are expected to father many children but are not raised to be responsible for supporting their children. Bodily flows are symbolic of social processes of flow in societies that depend on sharing. "Individual pathologies, caused by disturbances in the flow of bodily substances, are mirrors of social pathologies caused by disturbances in the flow of mutual support and aid" (Sobo 148). According to folk belief, women can become ill from unexpelled semen that hasn't contributed to forming a baby; from a "backlog of blocked decomposing menses" resulting if a condom gets stuck in the vagina; or from a "false belly" caused by sorcery (Sobo 151). A sick belly is an indication of a sick relationship that fails in the "flow of mutual support."

According to Trinh T. Minh-ha, in many parts of Africa, the word " 'belly' refers to the notion of occult power," which resides in the woman's belly (Trinh 1989: 136). Indeed Ella's belly has tremendous revolutionary potential evidenced by the damaging storm it generates. Thus Ella is associated with the powerful yet voiceless "damned witch Sycorax" of *The Tempest*, mother of Caliban who was banished for her sorcery (Shakespeare 1987: 51). When women's magic of creating life, healing and storytelling became a threat to men, they appropriated this function and excluded women from "magico-religious functions," labeling magic women as witches (Trinh 1989: 129).

Folklore and oral tradition are an antidote to the printed colonial knowledge that has zombified the colonized and the patriarchal knowledge that has disempowered women. Throughout the novel, Brodber uses dialect, folklore and other examples of oral tradition to suggest that the recovery of spirit is achieved by recovering these oral traditions. She acknowledges the complexity of Jamaican language, which has been described as a "continuum, one end of which is standard English, the other a Creole dialect comprised of English- and African-derived words within an African linguistic structure" (Chevannes 1998: 102). Many stories, such as those about slave revolts, exist mainly in oral tradition. Brodber has researched the use of oral tradition in social history and her novel suggests that the half not told would be the half that is not preserved in print and must be recovered from fragments of oral tradition.[3] If print can separate soul from body, oral tradition can reembody the story and disclose the history of resistance to oppression.

Upward social mobility in Jamaica requires the shedding of the old skin of early socialization: mother tongue, mother culture, mother wit—the feminized discourse of voice, identity and native knowledge. (Cooper 1993: 3)

The tales are one of the places where the most subversive elements of our history can be safely lodged. . . . These tales encode what is overtly threatening to the powerful into covert images of resistance so that they can live on in times when overt struggles are impossible or build courage in moments when it is. (Sistren 1986: xv)

By allowing Ella's body to "speak," Brodber restores spirit to body and exemplifies oral tradition as an alternative to the disembodied discourse of the colonizer. This challenges the patriarchal transformation of bodily texts into psychoanalytic or anthropological master narratives. Ella reminds us of Breuer's hysteria patients such as Bertha Pappenheim, known as Anna O., who "regressed from the symbolic order of articulate German to the semiotic level of the body and the unintelligibility of foreign tongues" (Hunter 1983: 474). Breuer and Freud translated and appropriated Bertha's body language and semiotic utterances into psychoanalytic theory just as Selwyn translated Ella's discourse into his play. Because Bertha eventually healed herself by becoming involved in social work, especially in protecting young girls from being sold into prostitution, Dianne Hunter asserts that Bertha's hysteria was a response to her social oppression as an intelligent woman denied educational and professional opportunities.

In patriarchal socialization, the power to formulate sentences coincides developmentally with a recognition of the power of the father. In this light, Bertha Pappenheim's use of gibberish and gestures as means of expression, can be seen as a regression from the cultural order represented by her father. (Hunter 474)

Thus Ella's utterance of "Mammy Mary's mulatto mule must have maternity wear" invokes both the Bertha of *Jane Eyre* and *Wide Sargasso Sea* and the Bertha/Anna O. of Breuer's analysis. Selwyn aka Rochester aka Breuer/Freud attempts to "civilize" Ella, however, she metamorphoses into Bertha, the madwoman in Rochester's attic and the hysteric in Freud's office. Thus as subaltern/hysteric, Ella does speak with her body. As Abena Busia states in her discussion of colonial women's silence, "for women, 'narrative' is not always and only, or even necessarily, a speech act" (Busia 1990: 104). Busia's remarks refer to the woman in Spivak's "Can the Subaltern Speak?" who waited until the onset of menstruation to commit suicide so that her suicide would not be interpreted as her response to an illicit pregnancy.

Bertha Pappenheim staged an hysterical childbirth, which suggests an attempt to give birth to her new identity, not confined by patriarchal restrictions. Similarly, Ella experiences a rebirth when she stages an hysterical pregnancy and generates a hurricane. Through her body's tempestuous discharge of waste, Ella speaks about the web of life and the ways that colonization violates nature as well as natives' bodies and minds. Her rebirth is effected by the return of the Jamaican folk knowledge that has been repressed by a patriarchal colonialism. If, as Hunter claims, "hysteria is feminism lacking a social network in the outer world," then Ella's hysteria indicates her need for a network of colonial resistance (Hunter 1983: 485).

After her healing, Ella is ready to join the community of people resisting colonialism, whose members identify themselves as farmyard animals. Reverend Simpson is Mr. Dan; Miss Gatha is Mother Hen; the necromancer is Master Willie; and Maydene is White Hen. *Myal* concludes with a discussion among these "animals" about decolonizing minds and spreading the consciousness of resistance. Ella has begun thinking about and questioning the negative message of the farm animal story. "Is that what I am to teach these children, Reverend Simpson? That most of the world is made up of zombies who cannot think for themselves or take care of themselves but must be taken care of by Mr. Joe and Benjie?" (Brodber 1988: 107). Brodber's characters use the terms "zombie" or "zombification" as metaphors for the process of colonization that deprives the colonized of the ability to think for themselves. Zombification is "not a case of awakening the dead, but a matter of the semblance of death induced by some drug known to a few. . . . It is evident that it destroys that part of the brain which governs speech and will power" (Hurston 1990: 196). Reverends Brassington and Simpson have a conversation about zombification, which Simpson explains as resembling the entire colonization process that deprives the colonized of their culturally constructed integrity: "People are separated from the parts of themselves that make them think and they are left as flesh only. Flesh that takes directions from someone" (Brodber 108).

When Ella begins to understand the story of Mr. Joe's farm she recognizes the insidiousness of this story in which the animals go on strike but find they are unable to feed themselves. She notices that the "actual message is never told," thus forcing the children to enter "into complicity" with the story by providing their interpretation that the colonized or subjugated people are unable to survive without their masters. However, the colonized or oppressed have often been quite capable of thinking for themselves in strikes and other acts of rebellion as in 1919, the year of Ella's fictional hurricane and a year when worldwide strikes, combined with other international events, offered an opportunity for social change throughout the world.

Colonial education teaches children the "negative lesson" that when the "animals" on Mr. Joe's farm strike for their rights, they're so dependent on Mr. Joe's protection that they have to return to his farm. However, the cause of the animals' dependency is that like Caliban, their knowledge of their natural world has been taken from them and Prospero's book knowledge has been denied them. In order to resist colonial zombification, the colonized must reclaim their natural knowledge and acquire just enough of the master's tools to use as an "antidote." Ella's hybrid ambiguity includes an ability to utilize oral traditions as well as print culture and allows her to pass for white and thus to infiltrate the master's discursive order and subvert it.

My people have been separated from themselves White Hen, by several means, one of them being the printed word and the ideas it carries. Now we have two people who are about to see through that. And who are these people, White Hen? People who are familiar with the print and the language of the print. (Brodber 109–10)

In order to reintegrate her black and white selves, her body and mind, Ella must use print and oral traditions and must reintegrate the history of her Irish and Jamaican ancestors, especially the history of resistance to British imperialism. As noted earlier, there are similarities in Britain's colonization of Ireland and Jamaica and the oppression of the Irish and Jamaican people under the British empire. There are also some significant connections between the resistance movements in Ireland and Jamaica. Certain historical events of 1919 are hinted at in the novel. For example, Ella's father was an Irish policeman, not an unusual role for the Irish in the British empire. In 1916, there was an unsuccessful uprising in Ireland. The majority of the Irish were opposed to the rising but after the leaders were brutally executed without trial by the British, the climate changed. In 1919 Sinn Fein declared an Irish Republic and thus began the twentieth-century's challenge to the British empire.

"Trade union development in Jamaica began in 1919 with the passage of a law that legalized trade unions and enabled them to conduct legal and financial affairs; . . . The 1919 law was a response to the postwar rash of strikes in Kingston and other ports, on sugar estates, and at cigar and match factories" (Kaplan et al. 1976: 79). In 1909, a "disgruntled civil servant, Sydney Cox, founded Jamaica's first nationalist organization, the National Club, and a newspaper, Our Own, showing the influence of the Sinn Fein Irish nationalists" (Kaplan et al. 77). Sinn Fein is Gaelic for "we ourselves" and it is the name for the most left-wing of the Irish nationalist political parties.

1919 was a year of labor unrest not only in Jamaica and elsewhere in the British empire but even beyond the empire. Yet significantly we hear nothing explicit about this in the novel, just as we hear little about these events in our history books—the half that is not told! 1919 uprisings in the British empire included strikes in Jamaica and Trinidad, riots in India for self-government, a general strike in Limerick and the Sinn Fein seizure of parliament in Ireland. A crack in the British empire was created by this chain of events in its colonies. The vibrations of this rupture resounded around the world that year, just as nature in Mass Cyrus' woods resonates to the vibrations of Ella's disease. There were similar events in the industrial countries including general strikes in Seattle and Winnipeg and a widespread climate of labor unrest in the United States, especially in the coal and steel industries, with 4 million American workers out on strike that year. There was a revolutionary strike in Berlin, and Lenin founded the Third International, which emphasized replacing wars between nations with an international class war.

Marcus Garvey, who was born in Jamaica, went to Harlem in 1916 to organize the first American black nationalist movement, which influenced the growing Rastafari movement in the 1950s in Jamaica. The dreadlocks of Ole African in *Myal* suggest the dreadlocks of Rastafaris. " 'When you are Dreadlocks you come like a outcast.' Locks had a shock value, but they were also a way of witnessing to faith with the same kind of fanaticism for which the prophets and saints of old were famous" (Chevannes 1994: 158). Dreadlocks or "matted hair" was also "symbolic of stepping beyond the control of the white-oriented society" (Chevannes 1998: 123). The Rastafari movement represents a synthesis of Christianity and African belief and resembles Myalism in its resistance to psychological colonization by recognizing the unique spiritual and cultural identity of the Caribbean people. Bob Marley and other reggae musicians have been influenced by the Rastafari movement, whose principal belief is in the divinity of Haile Selassie, Ras (prince) Tafari Makonnen, Emperor of Ethiopia 1930–1975. "Their messages are rooted in their despair of dispossession, their hope is in an African or diasporan solution. As a result their messages emerge as an ideology of social change" (Brodber and Green 1981: 26).

By embracing their traditional culture as expressed in reggae music, dub poetry or in contemporary revivals like the Rastafari movement, Jamaican people can regain confidence in themselves especially in their ability to manage their lives and their country. Ella's "tempest," which alludes to the spirit thievery of Prospero in Shakespeare's play, is a metaphor for the spiritual, cultural and political expressions of resistance in the twentieth century from the 1919 strikes and the pan-Africanism of Garvey to the Rastafari, and the validation of "vulgar" Caribbean culture in literature like Brodber's, reggae music and other contemporary forms of oral tradition. "Erna Brodber's narrative method exemplifies the interpenetration of scribal and oral literary forms: a modernist, stream-of-consciousness narrative voice holds easy dialogue with the traditional teller of tales, the transmitter of anansi story, proverb, folk song and dance" (Cooper 1993: 3).

To understand *Myal*, we must read beyond the text into a recovery of oral traditions about slave rebellions and reggae songs alluding to decolonization. In her article on oral sources, Brodber emphasizes the importance of recovering history from the perspective of the oppressed by using oral tradition. She gives an example of using oral sources about a slave rebellion to reveal how the slaves felt about this event. Citing Trinidad author V. S. Naipaul, who asks whether historians should tell the story of the slave trade "as if it were just another aspect of mercantilism," Brodber challenges the new historian to abandon detachment and incorporate emotion into historical accounts (Brodber 1983: 7). If the printed word is one method by which "people have been separated from themselves," then recovering oral traditions, whether folklore or folk religions like Myal, can heal and restore the colonized psyche (Brodber 1988: 109). Generations later, the possibilities for change suggested by the events of 1919 are being realized as expressed by a woman's oral history, describing changes since her grandmother's time, that was published by a collective of working-class Jamaican women:

In the sixty years or so between her birth and mine, history had given me the space to be angry about her subservience to an unjust system. Since her birth, women had won the right to vote, Marcus Garvey had challenged racism, the Russian Revolution had taken place, and the British Empire had fallen. (Sistren 1986: 197)

NOTES

1. Ella flies because she identifies with the texts she has been reading, such as Peter Pan, in which the characters fly. She also flies because she is associated with Ariel, the spirit in *The Tempest*. See Roberto Fernandez Retamar, "Caliban: Notes towards a Discussion of Culture in Our America" for a discussion of Ariel as the postcolonial intellectual. "There is no real Ariel-Caliban polarity: both are slaves in the hands of Prospero. . . . But Caliban is the rude and unconquerable master of the island while Ariel, a creature of the air, although also a child of the isle, is the intellectual" (Retamar 1974: 28). In Césaire's *Une Tempête*, Ariel is a mulatto like Ella. Also see Edward Kamau Brathwaite, "Caliban, Ariel and Unprospero in the Conflict of Creolization: A Study of the Slave Revolt in Jamaica in 1831–32."

2. See Edward Kamau Brathwaite, *The Development of Creole Society in Jamaica, 1770–1820* and Françoise Vergès, "Creole Skin, Black Mask: Fanon and Disavowal."

3. See Erna Brodber, "Oral Sources and the Creation of the Social History of the Caribbean."

4
~ No Country for Young Men ~

I am the woman
in the gansy-coat
on board the *Mary Belle*,
in the huddling cold,
holding her half-dead baby to her

"Mise Éire," Boland 1990: 79

Eavan Boland, the author of "Mise Éire," creates poetry that describes the
historical problems of Irish women like this immigrant mother, just as the
authors of all four novels address the problems of women living in difficult
historical contexts. In Boland's poem "Mise Éire," a scar is a metaphor for
the often unfinished healing of the wounds that people, especially women,
survive. "A new language is a kind of scar and heals after a while into a pass-
able imitation of what went before" (Boland 1990: 79). *A Kind of Scar* is also
the title of Boland's essay on the necessity of Irish women poets representing the realities of Irish women despite the tendency of Irish male poets to
use women as an icon representing the Irish nation. Boland recognized this
difficulty of writing authentically as an Irish woman through her chance
meeting with an Achill woman who talked to her about the strength of the
people who survived the famine. Referring to poems by Irish male poets
that represent the nation as Dark Rosaleen or Kathleen Ní Houlihan,
Boland sees this as a dangerous process not only because it erases the reality
of women's lives but also because it erases the reality of Irish history.
"Women were part of that wrath, had endured that grief. It seemed. . .[an]
insult that at the end of all, in certain Irish poems, they should become ele-

ments of style" (Boland 1989: 12). The mythic or emblematic usage of women in such poems renders the historical suffering of Ireland as abstract as the historical suffering of Irish women.

> Past or present, there is a human dimension to time, human voices within it and human griefs ordained by it. Our present will become the past of other men and women. We depend on them to remember it with the complexity with which it was suffered. (Boland 24)

The two main female characters in Julia O'Faolain's *No Country for Young Men* experience real pain as a result of the complex interrelationship of cultural and historical forces involved in the degradation of Irish women, including Irish Catholicism's monastic fear of female sexuality and nationalist extremists' glorification of male-dominated terrorism. O'Faolain also reveals the personal impact of the psychological and economic violence of colonialism that degraded the Irish, damaging self-esteem and familial relationships and resulting in problems of alcoholism and domestic abuse. When Gráinne first appears in the novel, she and her son, Cormac, are returning home from the shelter for battered women to which she has fled to escape her husband Michael's alcoholism. Throughout the novel, Gráinne is haunted by reminders of Ireland's history of famine, poverty and colonization, and her great-aunt Judith, a nun, is one of these reminders.

A few years ago I finally visited Ireland. None of my Irish relatives had ever returned or expressed any desire to return there and I understood why. Raised in the home of my Irish maternal grandmother in an Irish-American community near Chicago, I heard about the horrors of immigration by steerage. My widowed mother feared we would end in the poor house, a fate that befell many Irish during the famine. Based on these transgenerational references, Ireland seemed a poor and sorrowful country. When I did go to Ireland, people often recognized my ancestry and talked about the famine and resulting diaspora. The innkeeper in my Dublin hotel made a remark that awakened me to the truth about my family and the diaspora Irish when he said, "The ones that had to leave took their bitterness with them." Thus some of the mysteries of my childhood began to unravel, among them that my grandmother's cupboards full of food in her basement were probably her insurance against famine.

Later while researching Irish history, I discovered that Sinéad O'Connor had arrived at the conclusion that alcoholism, domestic abuse and other conditions in the Irish family are the effects of years of colonial oppression. O'Connor observed that there is a transgenerational wound resulting from the failure to mourn the mid-nineteenth century famine and diaspora and wrote a song about this entitled "Famine." O'Connor, who was abused by her mother, has stated in interviews that she believes the frequency of domestic problems and even child abuse in Ireland can be attributed to its history of colonization, the physical suffering due to the British policies that caused starvation and the psychological suffering due to the repressive role of the Catholic Church toward women and sexuality. Sinéad O'Connor, in her unruly desire to break the silence about the psychological damage of colonialism, resembles the unruly women characters in O'Faolain's novel.

I have compared Ireland in the song to a child who has been tortured—spiritually, sexually, physically, psychologically and emotionally. When a child experiences this type of horror, in order to survive she drives herself outside her body, so as not to feel what is too painful to feel . . . so we try everything to make the feelings go away: drugs, alcohol, food, sex, money, anger, suicide. (Sinéad O'Connor, quoted by Waters, *Irish Times*, 10/11/94)

Studies of survivors of the Jewish Holocaust and their children validate this interpretation of the psychological effects of devastating events such as the Holocaust and the Great Famine in which whole families and communities were destroyed. The Irish language and culture virtually disappeared during the famine because of the widespread death and immigration. "There are both qualitative and quantitative factors in the limitations on what can be dealt with through mourning. The quantity or quality of losses may be beyond one's capacity to integrate, e.g., when in the case of the Holocaust one's entire people and civilization perished" (Krystal 1991: 104). As the one hundred fiftieth anniversary of the famine approached, John Waters of the *Irish Times* attempted to uncover this repressed memory because he believes we are doomed to repeat what we refuse to remember. In an opinion article, he states that psychiatrists have confirmed his theory that repression of painful experiences can apply to collectivities as well as to individuals: "In the past I have put it to psychiatrists that what is true of individual people might also be true of peoples, of societies, of nations. The answer I have received has invariably been yes" (Waters, *Irish Times*, 10/11/94).

As Waters suggests in this article and in a later article, "Why the Ex-slave Sounds Like the Oppressor," until they recover the history and acknowledge the impact of oppression, victims will often identify with the oppressor. Rather than having compassion for those who still suffer the consequences of colonization, the ex-slave may instead judge them as harshly as the British judged the nineteenth-century famine Irish. The background to the famine includes the economic system established by British colonization in which the Anglo-Irish, often absentee landowners owned most of the land and had the power to evict their subsistence level tenants. This system functioned only because the peasants had the cheap and nutritious potato as a food staple, though some authorities realized that the poor had no recourse should the potato crop fail. The potato blight that caused the Great Famine began in 1845 and continued until 1849, causing at least one and a half million people to starve and another two million to emigrate between 1845–1852. "The Famine and its aftermath laid bare the huge gulf that lay between Ireland, largely inhabited by a poverty-stricken population living constantly on the edge, with no rights of land ownership, and the United Kingdom of which it was supposed to be a part" (Litton 1994: 8).

Concerned that nationalist versions of Irish history, especially famine and postfamine, had been constructed to serve the purpose of creating a national identity and an Irish nation, historians formed historical societies in Northern Ireland and in the Republic expressly to deconstruct the separatist myth of Ulster loyalism and the nationalist myth of the Republic. However, this revisionist approach, which influenced the writing of Irish history for several decades, has in turn been challenged by postrevisionist historians who dispute the possibility of creating value-free history and complain that the academic objective tone of revisionist history desensitized "modern historical writing to the sufferings and injustices of Ireland's past" (Brady 1994: 10). James Donnelly's "The Construction of the Memory of the Famine in Ireland and the Irish Diaspora 1850–1900" compares revisionist histories and nationalist versions of famine history to popular memory of these events as recorded in oral histories by the Irish Folklore Commission in 1945. Donnelly recognizes that the nationalist version often corresponds to the oral accounts, representing a different truth, another meaning that reflects the emotional impact of the famine on popular memory and the resentment toward the insensitive and even racist British press coverage of the famine and its aftermath. The *London Times*, for example, had rejoiced that as a result of the famine "a Celtic Irishman will be as rare in Connemara as is a Red Indian on the shores of Manhattan" (Donnelly 1996: 45).

This background on Irish history and contemporary debates about long-term consequences of colonization are relevant to my discussion of *No Country for Young Men* because Julia O'Faolain's novel alludes to this repressed history in its motifs of famine, diaspora and the slave mind. The psyche of Judith, a nun who is the great-aunt to Gráinne in the novel, is a battleground of contesting nationalist and revisionist versions of history. Judith, who also suggests the subaltern voice of oral tradition and fairy tales, is struggling to break a male-imposed silence after years of being forcibly kept in a convent. Gráinne, who tries to help Judith, is having an affair that she hopes will enable her to escape a lifeless marriage. Her lover is James, a yank who has come to Ireland to work on a film about Sparky Driscoll, another American who came to Ireland in 1922 and "got himself killed by Orangemen in the North" (O'Faolain 1980: 40).

An important theme in O'Faolain's novel is that marginalized or scapegoat characters, such as Judith and Patsy, an aging Republican extremist who works for the Grateful Patriots Youth Club, enact the repressed violence under the surface of Irish society. Fear of the stigma of colonization might cause the postcolonial elite of Ireland to project this stigma onto the poor or otherwise marginal members of society. Those who historically were colonized may feel haunted by the representational pit of inferiority constructed for them by the colonizer. Thus they may find someone within their society or their family to scapegoat so that they can identify with the colonizer rather than the victim. However, those who have tried to ignore their history, such as James and Gráinne, are at risk of being engulfed and destroyed by the return of the repressed, which keeps surfacing.

The Irish legend of Gráinne and Diarmuid, a love triangle that ends in violence,[1] is the framework through which this theme is developed in the novel. The first version of this triangle takes place during the civil war fought for the Irish Republic in 1922. Sparky Driscoll is sent to Ireland on behalf of an Irish-American group that is providing financial support for Ireland's fight against British colonialism. Sparky flirts with Kathleen and her sister Judith and is eventually killed by Judith, who realizes he intends to expose the misuse of American money. The second version of the legendary story occurs in 1979 when Irish-American James Duffy is sent on behalf of another group interested in making a documentary to "raise funds for the Irish Republican cause" (O'Faolain 1980: 33). James has an affair with Gráinne, named after the mythical Gráinne, great-niece of Kathleen and Judith. He discovers and may reveal Judith's secret but is killed by Patsy, a confused old man on the fringe of the Irish Republican Army (IRA), who wants to prevent the breakup of Michael and Gráinne's marriage.

O'Faolain represents Judith and Patsy, the two characters who commit these murders, as damaged souls. "Patsy's sickness was of the soul and chronic" (O'Faolain 360). Both characters have been marginalized by their families and psychologically violated by their indoctrination with colonial, nationalist and terrorist ideologies. Patsy has been subjected to the invasive tactics of police interrogation in an attempt to make him talk about the IRA and Judith to shock treatments used to silence her about Sparky's murder in order to safeguard the Republic's reputation. The minds of both characters resemble the bog, a significant motif in the novel. One meaning of the bog, as it relates to these two socially marginal characters, is to suggest the return of the repressed. This is best expressed by Gráinne's response to James's query about where the Irish stand on the IRA:

In practical terms we're dead against them, but in some shady, boggish area of our minds there's an unregenerate ghost groaning "up the rebels." Most of us keep the ghost well suppressed, but children, drunks, unemployable men, and emotional misfits can become possessed by it. (O'Faolain 199)

Just as the British colonizer made the Irish his scapegoats, so the postcolonial Irish elite may scapegoat the socially marginalized such as Patsy and Judith. Like Judith, Patsy was not entirely all right even before being subjected to the mental and physical abuses of prison. As a child, Patsy had "always been slow physically . . . and then there was that something—what?—about him that made people snigger behind his back and pick him last when they were making up teams" (O'Faolain 263). Similarly, Kathleen says to her sister Judith, "You're childish . . . people that are good at the books are often oddly stupid when it comes to practical things" (O'Faolain 322). Thus the childish Patsy and Judith as well as Gráinne's son, Cormac, are those most influenced by IRA propaganda in the novel. Yet as Gráinne herself admits, it is perhaps only more successful repression that differentiates her from the "childish" and emotionally confused characters who express political sentiments that other characters repress. Thus O'Faolain's novel seems to warn that, until the repressed side of Irish history, including patriarchal oppression of women, colonialism and anticolonial violence is examined openly, there is the danger of this rejected material returning in sporadic eruptions of violence.

The repressed history is represented by metaphors of Dracula, vampires and cannibalism. The American, James, refers to people he sees in the pub: "All around him were Draculas, Bugs Bunnies and hay-rake grins" (O'Faolain 66). During the civil war, old women refer to young women who encourage men to die for nationalism, as "Vampires" (O'Faolain 129). Because colonization invades boundaries—geographical, cultural and psychological—it creates a potentially unstable and ambiguous relationship between the colonized and the colonizer. In *No Country for Young Men*, there is an example of this in the story of Timmy, who is a great house servant and "bum-lover" of the Anglo-Irish landlord. When Judith takes Sparky to see the house, Timmy tells them that like a mouse, " 'I nibble because I love, as the cannibal said to his girl friend. Mind you, it's a two-way act. I too,' said Timmy, and postured, 'am devoured' " (O'Faolain 290). He states that the current landlord's father voted against Home Rule because the landlords "love" the Irish so much that they would rather kill them than give them independence.

In his article, "The Occidental Tourist: Dracula and the Anxiety of Reverse Colonization," Stephen Arata examines *Dracula* as an occidental tourist narrative about the imperialist "anxiety of reverse colonization." Bram Stoker, who was born in Ireland, must have been aware that "Britain's subjugation of Ireland was marked by a brutality often exceeding what occurred in the colonies" (Arata 1990: 633). Narratives such as *Dracula* exhibit unconscious motives of alleviating cultural guilt over the damaging impact of British imperialism and relieving fears that the victimized will become the victimizer.

For Stoker, the Gothic and the travel narrative problematize, separately and together, the very boundaries on which British imperial hegemony depended: between civilized and primitive, colonizer and colonized, victimizer (either imperialist or vampire) and victim. (Arata 626–27)

This fear of reverse colonization, or becoming like the other, dates from the time of Edmund Spenser, who inhabited Ireland for awhile during the early stages of British colonization. He addressed this problem of the colonizer adopting the barbarous customs of the Irish in his polemical *View of the Present State of Ireland*: "The English that were are now much more lawless and licentious than the very wild Irish. . . . That seemeth very strange which you say, that men should so much degenerate from their first natures as to grow wild" (Spenser 1970: 63). From the sixteenth century to the present, representations of the Irish as barbarous, crazy or grotesque safeguard the civilized status of colonizers or neocolonizers. As a traveler in Ireland in 1860, Charles Kingsley described the Irish peasants as "white chimpanzees" (Hirsch 1991: 1119). During the Victorian era, there was a conviction in England and Scotland that the Irish were inherently inferior and unfit to manage their own affairs. Representations of the Irish "Paddy looked far more like an ape than a man. In less than a century, Paddy had become a monstrous Celtic Caliban capable of any crime known to man or beast" (Curtis 1971: 29). The shift into this simian or apish Celt was a result of increased resistance by the Irish to the injustices under British rule, and the changes in "Paddy's features during the middle decades of the century do seem to reflect a change in attitude among many Victorians about Irishmen and Irish agitation" (Curtis 29).

Even recent anthropological studies of Ireland have misrepresented the Irish. Scheper-Hughes is a contemporary anthropologist who conducted a study of rural Ireland entitled *Saints Scholars, and Schizophrenics* (1979), which revealed family secrets about mental illness and sexual repression that were hurtful to the people who had trusted her. The *Irish Times* criticized her for this betrayal of trust noting that the "American anthropologists who write books about the cultural death-rattles of the 'peasants' of western Ireland have not always tried very hard to disguise the locations in which they lived, probed and eavesdropped" (Viney 1980: 12). The people who trusted her, fed her and helped when her child was sick were shocked to find that she had revealed the darkest secrets of their souls, which she "dissects and holds up to the light. She was a skillful pathologist of human nature" (Viney 12). Eventually, Scheper-Hughes came to recognize the insensitivity of her report on these rural people and discussed it in an article comparing her fieldwork among rural Irish and Pueblo Indians. What, as a young and eager anthropologist, she had once misunderstood as uncooperative dissimulation, Scheper-Hughes later understood in light of a people's resistance to centuries of oppression: "Just as the rural Irish took their masses into private homes and their Irish language into secret schools to protect them, so the Pueblos took their religious and ceremonial life underground into the kivas" (Scheper-Hughes 1987: 71).

When Gráinne first notices James looking at her, she wonders if his gaze is an anthropologist's or a tourist's. Her speculation on James's gaze evokes the above- mentioned history of tourist and ethnological narratives scrutinizing the Irish. Indeed James's thought process demonstrates his tendency to distance himself against the danger of going native by assuming the role of tourist or anthropologist. Clearly James has romanticized Ireland. "The long passion of Irish history mystified him, though he had opened himself to the local geography. . . . Dublin struck him as cryptic" (O'Faolain 1980: 168). He admits that despite the "haphazard nature of his arrival here . . . he was seeing Dublin as an ancestral womb" (O'Faolain 168).

James's journey to Ireland is both a research project and a romantic quest for escape from a tedious marriage and unemployment in California. James at times confuses both women, especially Gráinne, with Ireland. His first reflections on Gráinne suggest she is more fantasy than reality. "It wasn't the woman qua woman who appealed to him, but the glimpse she was giving him of alien lives. He was the demon in an old story . . . who lifts the roofs of houses and looks inside" (O'Faolain 106). He later wonders if the Irish might feel things more strongly and "peeps" into their lives to find out. "He was ready to believe that a repeatedly defeated island, throttled by ancient and fermented rages, might be the place to breed passions of a transporting magnitude" (O'Faolain 144). Contemplating his affair with Gráinne, James thinks in terms of "letting himself hope for some dream of wholeness or newness, for some change in his way of being such as old Celtic ladies had a way of offering men who let themselves be lured on strange trips" (O'Faolain 170–71). In the next breath, he is wondering whether the aunt could be a "Celtic seer or one of those sly old hags whose knowledge could be of use" (O'Faolain 171). Like Irish geography and history, both Judith and Gráinne seem cryptic to him, bearers of some secret wisdom that his penetrating voyeuristic gaze will discover. For all his fascination with this romantic fantasy of Irish women, James is unable to truly comprehend Ireland. Not only does he need Gráinne's help to translate the dialect of some interviewees but he also can't entirely understand the story that he records from Judith, or its broader implications.

However, James's encounters with the Irish are disturbing as well as enchanting. The ancestral quality of Dublin is not entirely reassuring because it confronts James with "deformed versions of his relatives back home" (O'Faolain 168). Though he has tried to enact a romantic fantasy about Ireland, James feels threatened with the grotesque appearances of people that surround him in the streets. "The tomato-complexion was not his but blazed like scar-tissue on the primitive, distant cousins whom he scrutinized daily in the Dublin streets" (O'Faolain 168–9). He sees Michael as a "friendly centaur" or a "lateral connection of one of Darwin's apes" (O'Faolain 204). This may be James's method of distancing himself, because this apelike husband surely couldn't suffer as a result of his wife's affair. It also evokes colonial simian images of the Celt. In his desire to be swept up in an exotic experience, James is a typical tourist, who is both attracted and repulsed by the strange ways of the natives.

James ponders this disturbing side of Ireland that he has seen in the pubs on his first night there. "Mangled features, worthy of a gallery of grotesques, blazing red skin, rheumy eyes—in one case the unmasked absence of an eye—tics and an absence of orthodontia registered like so many reminders of mortality" (O'Faolain 105). Earlier that day in the hotel bar, he first notices the "primitive" toothwork of the Irish. Are the Irish really more primitive than Americans or is this the signature of deprivation, poverty and malnutrition that resulted from centuries of British colonization? O'Faolain's technique for exposing the impact of long-term oppression is subtle. After Patsy tries to warn him away from Gráinne, James describes this strange visitor to her as not very tall. Gráinne explains that Patsy's short stature is the result of dietary deficiency and that "[n]obody in the movement is tall . . . they're undernourished" (O'Faolain 221).

On the boat returning to Ireland, Gráinne had wondered if the children's "carnival greed" might have its origins in "some memory of famine days" (O'Faolain 57). Gráinne has problems dealing with the poverty and suffering that surrounds her and which causes her to feel guilt for her relatively privileged life. As she interprets the tapes, Gráinne comments that she can't stand to hear the complaining of the men James interviewed: "Dere were no jobs and any dere were went to de boys who'd accepted de traty" In response James tells her, "You're not living on the breadline" (O'Faolain 208). Gráinne's desire to escape the threat of falling into the abjection around her is represented by a recurring dream. "In dreams sometimes she rode that coldly perilous, ravishing wooden horse and hoped that it might take off from the merry-go-round and become a Pegasus" (O'Faolain 294). Literally, this dream is a reference to a childhood incident when she first experienced the resentment of the Irish poor toward her and other members of the newly risen elite that replaced the Anglo-Irish. When she was six and on vacation with her family, Gráinne went out alone for a carousel ride. The ride attendant terrified her by refusing to stop the carousel and she realized that he was punishing her parents through her. She understood in childhood that the poor, in particular the family servants like the maids who wouldn't stop tickling her, hated her family. "They hadn't minded working for the old stock, but working for their own kind stuck in their gullets" (O'Faolain 295).

Gráinne thinks that the recent recurrence of this dream is about her affair with James. "Sex was the merry-go-round. She did and didn't want to get off. The attendant was now inside herself" (O'Faolain 294). However, her affair with James is not solely about sex any more than Kathleen's flirtation with Sparky was. Like her predecessor Kathleen, Gráinne wants an escape from the suffering around her, the suffering of the present as well as the recurring cycles of suffering in Irish history. After she leaves James's hotel room, she encounters a parking attendant with an "anonymous working-class face: red, bunched, prematurely old . . . unemployment in the country was rocketing. She felt herself a parasite" (O'Faolain 256). Perhaps if Gráinne can escape through an affair or by going to California, she won't be haunted by the ghosts of the past or the faces of carnival ride or parking lot attendants that arouse her feelings of guilt.

Obviously, Gráinne is not responsible for this suffering but the legacy of colonization combined with Catholicism's focus on guilt has left her with this diffuse sense of shame. She also feels guilty for hurting her husband through this love affair. Thus although both James and Gráinne might at times feel threatened by the poverty and other problems of Ireland and the fragile middle-class distinction between themselves and the poor, Gráinne is more vulnerable than James. He can return to California and leave this adventure behind him without suffering the same emotional losses of family and country. Gráinne, with her familial and cultural roots in Ireland, is deeply attached to Michael because they are cousins and have always known each other. The cultural influences that Michael and Gráinne share include the history of colonization, Irish nationalism and the Catholic religion.

While the colonizer castrated the colonized Irish male, it is the colonized Irish female who was blamed for this betrayal, especially if she dared to challenge male authority. History lessons remind her that it was a "[w]oman's frail morals which led to the English first coming here," a reference to Dervorgilla whose infidelity in the twelfth century forced her lover to flee to England and seek help from Henry II, thus resulting in England's invasion in 1169 (O'Faolain 34; Weekes 1990: 184). This historical guilt of Irish women is the source of Gráinne's anxiety about her relationship with both husband, Michael, and son, Cormac. Has she damaged Cormac psychologically either because of her affair with James or because of the incident when she accidentally caught his testicles in a zipper? When this occurred, Michael began "trembling, unnerving her and yelling that females brought up in convents were unfit to be let near male children" (O'Faolain 235). As she remembers this incident and the fear that she may have "maimed him for life," Gráinne worries that the patriotic ballads and stories she told her son may have influenced his fascination with the IRA. She also wonders if it is her fault that Michael has lost the sexual libido he evidently exhibited with his previous lover. As a result of colonialism, Irish monastic misogyny and the IRA's eroticization of violence, the primary options open to Irish men in O'Faolain's novel are Michael's passivity and retreat into alcoholism and Owen Roe's machismo stance of aggressive political leadership. Though Irish men's problems described in the novel are a result of the combined colonial and Catholic conditioning rather than the fault of Irish women, internalized colonialism not only makes the oppressed self-destructive but also makes them blame themselves for the problem rather than the entire degrading process of colonial occupation and dispossession.

Until recently, Catholicism has caused restrictions on birth control and divorce in Ireland and thus already impoverished families may have had more children than they could support, often a contributing factor to domestic problems. The Catholic religious ideology that stresses woman's purity and sexual repression was perhaps exaggerated in Ireland by the influence of colonialism and the convergence of religious ideology with a reality of hardship and suffering. Gráinne contemplates how prayers programmed her adolescent passion for a suffering Christ as Divine Lover, "Blood of Christ inebriate me. Water from the side of Christ wash me. . . . Within thy wounds hide me" (O'Faolain 157). When Judith tells a nun of her dream of a man who "held his guts in his hand," Sister Gilchrist says, "Now that would remind you of the statue of Christ showing his sacred heart" (O'Faolain 10). Gráinne, worrying about the absence of religious statues in Judith's room, supposes she will have to buy a Sacred Heart "drawing aside his robe to reveal an organ bleeding solid pigment for our sins" (O'Faolain 91). These descriptions suggest an eroticization of suffering. Revolutionary politics and Catholic doctrines also converged in the heroic figure of Padraig Pearse. Pearse, who was executed for his role in the 1916 Easter rising, invoked the model of Christ's crucifixion in his philosophy of revolutionary bloodshed. "Padraig Pearse was a prime example for he died hamming to his script which then became unassailable. . . . He was inspired by the mass, a daily sacrifice, as every Irishman knows" (O'Faolain 66).

Gráinne shrewdly wonders whether Owen Roe's mother's cancer wasn't the result of "swallowed rage at all those Hail Marys," and she imagines the knowledge of her betrayal of her husband is "secret as a cancer" (O'Faolain 150, 241). Gráinne's mother also died of cancer and her fear of inheriting it necessitates frequent visits to the gynecologist. Her reflections equate the psychological violation of the confessional with the sexual violation of the gynecological exam.

Gráinne, an ex-Catholic, had transferred the odium she might have felt for priests on the medical men. . . . Terrified of her heredity, she had to go regularly to a gynecologist who poked lubrified fingers inside her vagina to take a smear test, exactly as her confessors, before she left the church, had poked spiritual probes into her head. (O'Faolain 98)

The bog is a central motif in *No Country for Young Men* because its ambiguity suggests both this repressed history of suffering and violence and the repressed threat of disorderly nature and women's sexuality. As a liminal space, the bog and fairy mounds, that are often located in bogs, are especially associated with the muddled mind of Judith and also the return of the repressed history. O'Faolain's adaptation of the bog motif combines Seamus Heaney's use of this motif in his poetry to signify the memory of Ireland's violent history with her use in association with unruly women. Heaney uses the bog motif in his poems "Bog Queen," "Grauballe Man," "Punishment" and "The Tollund Man" to suggest the ancestral historical memory. Yet like many Irish male authors, Heaney attributes Ireland's violent history to the bloodthirsty goddess of sovereignty.

There is an indigenous territorial numen, a tutelary of the whole island, call her Mother Ireland, Kathleen Ní Houlihan, the poor old woman, the Shan Van Vocht, whatever . . . who needed new bridegrooms each winter to bed with her in her sacred place, in the bog, to ensure the renewal and fertility of the territory in the spring. Taken in relation to the tradition of Irish political martyrdom for that cause whose icon is Kathleen Ní Houlihan, this is more than an archaic barbarous rite: it is an archetypal pattern. (Heaney 1980: 57)

The feminized bog thus represents the historical memory of repeated invasions and an ambiguity toward violence as an abhorrent, yet comprehensible, resistance to invasion. Seamus Heaney's poetry reveals an intimate knowledge of the consequences of psychological and physical violence related both to colonization and the resistance to recent colonial occupation in Northern Ireland. However, he elides the historical realities in deference to archetypal, barbarous customs of the prehistoric fertility goddess.

In fact, Cheryl Herr, in "The Erotics of Irishness," challenges the Irish nationalists' notion of the bloodthirsty Mother Goddess as the cause of violence and proposes rather that the refusal to recognize Ireland's "female-identified" prehistory has produced an imbalance that generated this negative archetype. Opposing violence in moralistic terms alone can't explain why "the oppressions of invading forces have been stylized through the centuries and introjected as the Dominatrix-Mound-Mother's putative pleasure in the death of her sons" (Herr 1990: 33). Nor can this limited approach explain the "neutralizing of sexuality" and the "schizophrenia that speaks in the voice of the body-censor" in Ireland (Herr 33).

Richard Kearney in his essay, "Myth and Motherland," attributes the association of Irish nationalism with blood sacrifice to the mythmaking of Yeats in particular, which enabled a symbolic transcendence of time and ergo of the class, religious and cultural differences within Ireland. He further suggests that the idealization of Irish womanhood is a compensatory gesture of elevation since the "women of colonized Ireland had become, in James Connolly's words, the 'slaves of slaves' " (Kearney 1984: 20). Kearney asserts that, as a people become dispossessed of their identity through colonization, they attempt to repossess an identity in the ideal or abstract realm. Thus as resistance to the English colonizer grew in the nineteenth and twentieth centuries, the image of Ireland as a "ravished virgin" was transformed into that of Ireland as a "militant mother goddess" (Kearney 21).

Julia O'Faolain adopts the notion of the bog as representative of the ambiguity of the Irish toward their history and toward female sexuality. In a country where women were expected to follow traditional roles within the family and use sex solely for reproduction, sexuality is dangerous and reminiscent of the fairy women that lure men into a timeless and apolitical realm. The sexuality of transgressive women like the mythic Gráinne and the novel's Gráinne exists outside the sphere of male control. In the heightened atmosphere of Ireland's patriotic resistance to colonization, Irish nationalists viewed the disruptive influence of unruly women on the male domain as a betrayal. The disorder of female desire is countered by the repression of eroticism in an atmosphere of political violence. O'Faolain's association of women with the bog motif symbolizes both the disorder of nature and the pagan disorder of pre-Christian Ireland.[2] According to Ann Weekes, O'Faolain's use of the bog is "similar in its relation to Showalter's 'wild' area of female experience, the bog, in its peripheral position between culture and totally untamed nature, also resembles the area that Sherry Ortner finds assigned to women 'outside and around' male culture" (Weekes 1986: 99).

Sexuality, for most of the novel's characters, has been displaced -for Michael to alcohol; for Patsy to political terrorism; and for Judith to her boglike, vaginal mind with its "power of suction" and "its unfathomable layers" (O'Faolain 1980: 12). Thus Judith's boglike mind, the repository of her repressed and displaced sexuality, is violated in lieu of her vagina by the male characters. Owen, Owen Roe, Michael, James and even Cormac all try either to repress or uncover her memory. When James first meets Michael O'Malley in a pub, O'Malley had apparently been offering to sell James his great-aunt. " 'To a Hollywood tycoon like yourself,' O'Malley had kept urging, 'it's small change. She's priceless' " (O'Faolain 63).

For O'Faolain, the bog represents not only Judith's colonized and sexualized mind but the colonized mind of Ireland and the Irish and a repository for repressed historical memory. Yet it is not only the original British colonial system that colonized the Irish mind with its alien language and ideologies but also a surviving residue of colonialism in the Republic that had learned to imitate the policies of its predecessor and maintain control over the population through nationalist ideologies and the oppression of women. The minds of all the characters have been colonized to one degree or another, resulting in a tendency toward self-abuse and self-censorship, but Judith and Patsy are those whose minds have been most susceptible to ideological violation, and in Patsy's case to British beatings, leaving them most capable of reproducing the latent violence by murdering the intrusive Americans. When her father criticizes her brother Eamonn for getting killed in the civil war, Kathleen responds, "That's the slave mind: always ready to condemn our own" (O'Faolain 72). Judith also thinks in these terms: "That was the value of the old struggles. They kept us from being slaves who assent to their servitude" (O'Faolain 76). Even Patsy expresses a similar sentiment when he says, "Sure they colonized our thoughts and minds. Took over our heads! It's hard to get free" (O'Faolain 86).

The novel's repetitions of the love triangle revise the original story of Diarmuid and Gráinne so that Sparky, as potential lover, is killed by Judith to protect her family from exposure and decades later James, as lover, is killed by Patsy to protect the marriage of Michael and Gráinne. Thus O'Faolain shows how the oppression of women in Irish culture is inter- twined with British colonial oppression and Catholic sexual repression. O'Faolain's seemingly grotesque characters, Patsy and Judith, have been damaged by this psychological violence of colonialism as well as the actual violence of the rebellion against this colonization. In such an atmosphere, love is a threat to the warlike mentality of an ongoing resistance to British colonization, and family relationships can enact the colonization process in which the psyche and the body of the colonized are violated by the colo- nizer.

Patsy explains that his inability to learn Gaelic is a result of his abuse in prison. While he served ten years for his IRA complicity, he was beaten about the head and force-fed during hunger strikes. Patsy tells Cormac, son of Michael and Gráinne, "It's easy to see you don't know what suffering does to the brain" (O'Faolain 186). Gráinne is concerned that Patsy is dan- gerous company for the young Cormac because of his Republican fanati- cism. "He was childish as a result of having been beaten round the head in a British gaol, where he had spent a number of years for planting bombs in Britain during the IRA campaign of the 1950s" (O'Faolain 87).

The sexual problems of Patsy differ mostly in degree from those of the other Irish male characters. He has never touched a woman and his knowledge of sex is limited to watching farm animals. As he pulls weeds outside Gráinne's window he thinks, "Weeds. Women. Concupiscence. Disorder" (O'Faolain 354). Yet his celibate misogyny resembles that of Kathleen's husband, Owen, who might have preferred a monastery but "was stuck with matrimony which he clearly suffered in a Pauline spirit" (O'Faolain 192). Nor does Gráinne's contemporary ex-lover, Owen Roe, have any sympathy for women. He tells Gráinne that her problem is a product of the nuns teaching girls that they "have the Holy Grail between their legs and some knight is going to come and find it" (O'Faolain 151). Gráinne's husband, Michael, thinks that Gráinne is unfaithful because he "[d]idn't fuck her enough. . . . Hard on a man when women got so demanding" (O'Faolain 305).

Although Patsy is critical of Gráinne's adulterous affair with James, he feels a strange sympathy for the passionate emotions he overhears during the couple's final tryst. "Yoked to the kind of feeling which was leaking through this house like gas, the act, Patsy had to admit, could be a way of escaping the mean limits of the self" (O'Faolain 360). Yet despite this momentary insight, Patsy is still more captivated by thoughts of death as a social event, a "gregarious word, for he thought of it not in terms of the lone grave but of the Day of Judgment which would be like a vast, exuberant political rally with all the old distinctions swept away and all mankind equal and fraternal" (O'Faolain 360).

Though Patsy has been damaged psychologically and physically, he is an ambiguous character, like most in this novel, and often acts the part of a wise fool. Despite his fear that he might have told on his mates as he was urged to do in the gaol, there is no indication that he ever turned informer and indeed he may have suffered the beatings for his resistance. Patsy is not too foolish to see the resemblance between the new Irish elite and the British colonizer. "Taking to the good life with as much gusto as the Brits ever did. Faces like Patsy's own. . . . Buggers who'd climbed over the corpses of their comrades, or whose fathers had, then turned into mirror-images of the old oppressors" (O'Faolain 219). Nor is he so naive as not to recognize the real threat of James's invasion into the secrets of other people's "cunts and countries." Another example of Patsy's insight is his remark connecting religious repression with political repression just as Gráinne connected gynecological violation with the confessional. "He'd gone to a clerical day-school and knew what it was to be regimented. . . . Through the confessional, they kept tabs on your inner life until you finally nerved yourself to damn your soul and defy them. When it came to organizational techniques the Republicans were nowhere in comparison" (O'Faolain 137).

Judith is constantly dismissed as mentally incompetent for trying to recall the secret of Sparky's murder yet she is the one to realize James has been murdered. Despite her alleged naive idealism as a young woman, Judith was aware that two forces, war and sex, set up a tension in her family. Even before she became unstable after the traumatic murder and her subsequent imprisonment in the convent, Judith's mind had been damaged by Catholic indoctrination and by IRA anticolonial politics. Her fear of sexuality is connected to the religious representation of women, especially the biblical Eve, as responsible for the origin of evil.

Judith's attraction to the cause of Irish liberation and a unified Ireland influence her nearly automatic response of killing Sparky when he threatens to denounce Owen. Judith's murder of Sparky had to be concealed because, if the American IRA supporters were to discover the murder, this would result in a loss of funding. Owen evidently decided that, to silence Judith, she should be forced to enter the convent and even to have shock treatments. He ignored her pleas to be released when she feared a breakdown. It is during his unyielding response to her appeal that she notes his clothes have a "clerical look" and his "face had grown more ascetic with the years" (O'Faolain 192).

Freud observed that women who exhibit hysteria are usually the ones who most aspired to be like men before puberty and then suddenly realized that opportunities for full participation in society are closed to them because of their gender. "The woman who expresses herself constitutes, as such, a danger in a society of men, for she has refused repression and, in so doing, refused to alienate herself in virile values. She will therefore be labeled mad" (Herrmann 1989: 71). Judith appears to be a woman whose abilities and behavior were not acceptable in the patriarchal Ireland of the 1920s. Judith's incarceration in a monastic cubicle is reminiscent of Patsy's imprisonment in a prison cell. In the convent she had no place of her own and no rights. "She had suffered then from the feeling that her space was being eroded" (O'Faolain 1980: 187). After years of incarceration in the convent and brainwashing by shock treatments, "compartments within her mind seemed to have collapsed, so that she could only with difficulty keep things separate. She sometimes confused everyday reality with what was only to be considered real in a spiritual sense" (O'Faolain 194). Judith's consciousness is constantly shifting between the past of the civil war and Sparky and the present IRA troubles and James.

Judith is suspicious that Cormac and others may be spying on her and at first distrusts James's recorder because this is a technique used in police interrogations. In an argument with Gráinne, James complains, "Words! the Irish are great with words! . . . They lie and deny. They skirmish and ambush. All your whole goddamn literature is about evasion" (O'Faolain 228). Yet if Gráinne and Judith are evasive, perhaps it is because they are aware of the possible danger of betrayal, a realistic concern evidenced by

James, who doesn't entirely understand what he has discovered by spying on Judith through the tape recorder and how dangerous its exposure could be. "My interest in the Sparky Driscoll story is purely as a story for our film. . . . Driscoll must have fallen foul of some elements within the Sinn Fein movement" (O'Faolain 319). Inadvertently, James would carelessly expose dangerous secrets of the people who trusted him and accepted him as a guest.

It is Judith who tells the story of the fairy mansion that arises from the bog and lures the traveler into a liaison with a fairy woman. While this story suggests a foreknowledge of James's fate, it also suggests the ability of males in the novel to enthrall females as well as vice versa. In reality, both Kathleen and Judith have felt enchanted by men. Kathleen tells Judith, "I'd like to rescue you before Owen sucks you into his madness. He's very powerful Owen is. Persuasive. Especially with women. I let him get me in thrall" (O'Faolain 332). It is difficult to tell whether Sparky really likes Judith or is simply flirting in order to manipulate her into revealing secrets as she fears, much as James's feelings toward Gráinne years later seem ambiguous and possibly mingled with his desire to uncover secrets. When Sparky kissed Judith, she felt that her body was out of control, besieged by waves of desire. In retrospect, Judith remembers the "treacherous way her own body had responded to Sparky's kiss" (O'Faolain 280). She then thinks about Sparky and her brother Seamus, while they are playfully engaged in male repartee, as both being capable of seducing and abandoning women and remembers these lines parodying a song: "My bonny lies over the ocean, and he's left me in the family way" (O'Faolain 233).

Judith's story about the dangerous repressed erotic realm of the fairy mound suggests the Other World, said to be ruled by women and linked to marginal, threshold places in the landscape. According to Angela Bourke, a woman could gain "privacy, prestige and sanction for subversions of her social role if she admitted or claimed to have been "away with the fairies" (Bourke 1995: 571). " 'Do you know the story,' she [Judith] asked the Principal Girl, [Gráinne] 'of the fairy mansion that rises from the bog at night. . . . And the traveller who enters is in danger of never escaping. If he eats fairy food' " (O'Faolain 1980: 283).

As mentioned earlier, from the time of Spenser, the colonizer has feared reverse colonization if the precolonial values pollute the colonial symbolic order. Similarly, the patriarchal symbolic order fears the power of the maternal body and female sexuality as suggested by the symbolism of the bog. The precolonial belief system encoded in the fairy mound and in meanings attributed to prehistoric dolmens is a potential repository for Cheryl Herr's "arkhein" conceptual space that restores the link between female body and landscape. Herr notes that in Ireland there has been a social and cultural repression of the body. She believes this predates and perhaps influences representations of Ireland as a mother who demands the sacrifice of her sons. Herr cites Scheper-Hughes's discovery of the prevalence of celibacy, "asceticism, resistance to being touched and sexual repression as well as . . . ignorance of orgasms among Irish countrywomen or the taboo on breast-feeding" and Rosita Sweetman's 1979 book that reports widespread ignorance about sexual matters (Herr 1990: 22). This alienation from the body was evidently not true of prehistoric Ireland in which mounds, cairns, tumuli and circular field monuments are "obvious features of Ireland as body" (Herr 7).

Like the fairy mound, the pagan bog, signifies "fallen nature" to the nuns but represents alternative and possibly nondualistic values outside of patriarchal or colonial rules. Fairytales represent the return of the repressed. Despite the Enlightenment, fairies continue to "carry off children and lovers, scamper naked and hairy in milkmaids' dreams, ride through the night sky, bewitch cattle and places and appear to old women as cats and toads" (Duffy 1972: 25). Fairyland is the realm of unconscious desires and loss and suggests a restoration of the fluidity Herr associates with the precolonial era, a fluidity that also acknowledges the ambiguities of a culture whose precolonial values and idioms are intermingled with those of the colonizer's culture. Herr uses the word "arkhein" to signify the different conceptual space that could be available to the Irish. Arkhein suggests "elements that might be variously expressed through ideas such as Kristeva's abject or semiotic or chora, Freud's Minoan moment, the primarily filmic sense of a nonpatriarchal imaginary, a (m)other tongue, the speaking of Luce Irigaray's 'two lips' " (Herr 1990: 8). The concept can counteract the representation of Ireland as a woman demanding male bloodshed, a myth that forecloses eroticism, and can restore a fluid pregendered, presymbolic alternative perspective.

The dolmens that, as Herr mentions, define the Irish landscape have long been known as the beds of Gráinne and Diarmuid in Irish oral tradition. The story of Gráinne and Diarmuid might originally have been a fertility story about the young woman as representative of the land requiring a young lover rather than an aging impotent one. However, in this already reversed patriarchal version, the young man is killed. In his book *Women of the Celts*, Jean Markale asserts that the remaining stories of powerful women, such as Gráinne or Deirdre, in Irish mythology are traces of a prepatriarchal tradition in which women take the "lead in everything right from the beginning" (Markale 1986: 209). "In celtic tales, it was the woman who rode by on a white horse and bade the man leap up behind her" (O'Faolain 1980: 170). One of the characteristics of the Gráinne story is the Irish "geis, a virtually untranslatable word, which can be passably rendered as 'prohibition,' 'taboo,' 'magic' and 'religious constraint' " (Markale 1986: 212). The geis has the power to counteract "society, laws and family ties" and to create a new perspective, "enabling the lovers to envisage an ideal, paradisiacal situation where all their dreams of childhood or intra-uterine life will come true" (Markale 237).

However, this "arkhein," paradisiacal experience can activate the male's anxiety of restoring the maternal universe wherein his subjectivity is threatened by absorption into a "whole that is greater than and necessarily more powerful than he" (Markale 227). Just as the erotic meaning of fairy mound stories is repressed so also is the erotic component in Newgrange. Even Gráinne in *No Country for Young Men* describes Newgrange only as a "pagan site where the Druids may have spilled human blood to renew the energies of the soil" (O'Faolain 1980: 214). An archaeologist's description of Newgrange, cited by Herr, evades its obvious symbolism as womb of re-birth, though his language reveals that significance: "Having wriggled through some difficult parts in the passage on my way in, my presence alone in the tomb—despite its massiveness—gave me a sense not of isola-tion, but of security" (Eogan's *Knowth and the Passage Tombs of Ireland*, quoted in Herr 1990: 27). In a response to Eogan's resistance to recognizing the womblike space of Newgrange, Herr then quotes an article by Irish art historian Dorothy Walker on the erotics of Newgrange: "The great tumulus at Newgrange . . . was originally built as a womb of the Mother Goddess, receiving the shaft of the rising sun directly into the spiral-carved interior at the winter solstice every year" (Walker, quoted in Herr 27). The repression of this relationship to earth monuments is not only a repression of women and sexuality but also of sensuality and even of the sacred or liminal alter-native reality as connoted by the Celtic Other World, a world that exists parallel to this world and intersects it at certain times of the year, especially Samhain or Halloween, when boundaries between the worlds dissolve. *No Country for Young Men* alludes several times to the dangerous and fascinat-ing Other World women who lure the hero into their timeless world to dis-appear forever.

The repression of eroticism and its replacement with male-dominated warfare is of course influenced by the history of colonialism and resistance to colonialism. The internalization of this process is seen through the psy-chology of the women characters in O'Faolain's novel, whose behavior is often oriented towards men or warfare. Judith aspires to be a revolutionary like the men, and the mostly Irish women in the battered women's shelter can't imagine living without a man regardless of how abusive he is. Of course until 1995, divorce was not an option in the Catholic Republic. When Gráinne considers her problems with Michael's alcoholism and the absence of sex, she realizes that she doesn't really want to end a marriage which is comfortable though unsuccessful. One of the women at the shelter, upon learning that Gráinne will return to her husband, says, "Ah well, strife's better than a lonely bed" (O'Faolain 1980: 61). In other words, some women in the shelter think that a bad marriage is preferable to being alone, which explains why these battered women often return to violent husbands as Gráinne has observed.

Gráinne is primarily focused on her relations with men and disconnected from other women in the novel. Indeed the central women characters in this novel seem unable to communicate with one another. Judith doesn't understand or sympathize with Kathleen's desire to escape the civil war and Ireland nor does Gráinne understand Judith's muddled attempts to communicate or her fear of her memories. The early loss of their mothers may signify Gráinne's and Judith's lost capacity for a matrilineal transmission of women's culture and community. On their first encounter, Judith is unintentionally revealing clues to Gráinne about the death of Sparky Driscoll and her fear of being silenced, committed or gaoled. At the same time, Gráinne's queries about these remarks arouse Judith's suspicion. Judith's desire to communicate is mingled with her fear of betrayal, as her brother-in-law Owen had repeatedly betrayed her. Eventually, Judith reenacts the murder of Sparky Driscoll. Gráinne "watched the old woman's fledgling movements. Jab went the old thing at a cushion, jab at the air" (O'Faolain 92). When Gráinne's husband, Michael, enters during this scene, Judith accuses Gráinne of trapping her and jabs Michael in the stomach with the hockey stick as she had bayoneted Sparky years earlier. "The girl's a stool pigeon. You won't catch me that easily. I deny it all" (O'Faolain 93).

Gráinne also fears the past. She thinks that Judith is like a "bundle of old things I thought I'd thrown out which suddenly turn up strewn around the place to shame me: the unwanted past" (O'Faolain 124). It seems Judith's aged flesh is repulsive not only on aesthetic grounds but also primarily as an indicator of the dangerous history encoded therein. Yet, gradually, sympathy for Judith begins to develop in Gráinne because she recognizes that Judith is a girl trapped in an "aged body." Gráinne realizes that Judith's secret puts her in danger from Owen Roe, who like the ancestral Owen wants to silence her. Naively, Gráinne believes that allowing James to tape-record Judith and keep the tape in some safe place would protect her aunt. She doesn't realize that James is self-serving enough to want to smuggle the tape out of Ireland with hope of a big story, not realizing, or perhaps not caring, that this story would endanger Judith. When Gráinne proposes to Judith that she be interviewed, Judith asks, "Would they put me in prison?" and warns "Don't breathe a word, girl . . . [e]specially to an American" (O'Faolain 116).

When Judith tries to tell her the story of the fairy mansion that arises from the bog at night and entraps the traveler, Gráinne thinks this indicates that Judith is just afraid of remembering, but fairy legends "constitute a marginal verbal art, subaltern discourse the opposite of the dominant modes of speech and thought . . . by which most privileged ideas are conveyed, especially in print" (Bourke 1996: 7). Perhaps Judith's story is intended as a warning against romantic deception. Both Sparky and James were Americans who may have had less interest in the women they seduce or attempt to seduce than in unmasking secrets. This obsession with uncovering secrets regardless of the consequences brings both men into dangerous boggy ground and causes their demise. The survivors of history remembering the past voluntarily differ from foreigners forcing an exposure of secrets without understanding the impact on the local context. James is deported because the government believes the film group is actually smuggling guns. However, his plane is turned back to Dublin because of weather and he returns to Gráinne's house. Patsy, who has been worried about James's violation of Judith's memory as well as his sexual "violation" of an Irish woman, decides to intervene and pushes James's car into the canal.

As the novel ends with Gráinne wandering along the canal looking for James, not realizing that he has been killed by Patsy, she resembles the banshee who wanders along canals wailing a warning of death. The bean sidhe who lures men into her timeless fairy mound realm has become the banshee, or supernatural wailing woman, who wails or laments to signify a death. Perhaps they and Gráinne are reminders of those Other World fairy mound women repressed by the patriarchy, Catholicism and colonialism, who return in folklore in association with mourning. This figure of the banshee suggests all the losses that Irish women have experienced since prepatriarchal times. They have not only lost the freedom to take sexual initiative but also a sense of community between women, which is now being restored through Irish feminism. In addition, the banshee image suggests mourning the human and cultural losses of the famine and the diaspora.

In traditional Irish mourning rituals, the "wailing women," like the banshees of folklore, occupy the liminal state between the "world of the living and the world of the dead" (Partridge 1980: 36). The characters of *No Country for Young Men* occupy a liminal place, where ghosts of the past mingle with the living. There are several references in the text to the threshold time of Halloween as well as to the already mentioned "between times" reality of the fairy world. " 'I'm afraid I'm between worlds,' she apologized. 'It's not Hallowe'en, is it? The souls of the dead seem to be about' " (O'Faolain 1980: 96). If Irish culture erases the body, as Herr claims, this represents avoidance of death as well as sexuality because the body implies both, as do womblike spaces such as Newgrange. Gráinne's body signifies the sexuality of young women and Judith's body signifies the abjection of aging women, thus both women represent the ongoing cycle of life and death.

As Ann Weekes observes, "Despite the loss of James, Gráinne has experienced existential freedom," realizing that her destiny is no longer determined by Irish history (Weekes 1986: 101). There was a difference between Gráinne's and James's perception of their love affair and this difference suggests that Gráinne is open to the arkhein and thus despite the loss of James, her life has changed irrevocably through this experience. She feels that their sexual affair is an experience of eternity being here now. "The seesaw of sexual play suited the indolent non-linear way she lived her life . . . she was ready to dance it again and again, like the participants in the set figures of an Irish dance who cover the same ground over and over, weaving back and forth, getting nowhere" (O'Faolain 227). James, on the other hand, wants to get somewhere, he wants to "freeze it" or control it, which is his undoing.

From her experience of hearing famine stories from an Achill woman, Eavan Boland realized how little she really understood Irish history because a simple glorification of the victories had erased the suffering, especially the suffering of women.

How had the women of our past—the women of a long struggle and a terrible survival . . . suffered Irish history and inscribed themselves in the speech and memory of the Achill woman, only to re-emerge in Irish poetry as fictive queens and national sibyls? (Boland 1989: 12).

In *A Kind of Scar*, Boland remembers that this Achill woman "kept repeating to me that they were great people, the people in the famine. Great people. I had never heard that before" (Boland 5). Like Boland, O'Faolain explores the impact of traumatic historical events on the lives of people, something that can be recaptured through oral tradition as well as literature.

Women's talk will indeed be harmless as long as women consider it trivial compared to talk with men. Women must turn to one another for stories; they must share the stories of their lives and their hopes and their unacceptable fantasies. (Heilbrun 1988: 44)

NOTES

1. Gráinne was to be married unwillingly to the old king of the Fiana, Finn mac Cumail. She first asked Oisin to run away with her and when he refused she turned to Diarmuid O'Duibne. When he also refused, she said, "I place upon you a geis of danger and destruction, O Diarmaid [Markale's spelling], unless you take me with you out of this house." So Diarmuid fled with Gráinne. Finn was angry and set off in pursuit, chasing them all over Ireland. When he finally finds them he tricks Diarmuid, who is killed by a boar. There are various versions of the ending in which Gráinne either returns to Finn, dies of grief, or enlists Diarmuid's sons in a fight against Finn (Markale 1986: 209–11).

2. For more discussion of the relationship of the bog to nature and the wildness of women, see Ann Weekes's article, "Diarmuid and Gráinne Again: Julia O'Faolain's *No Country for Young Men.*" Also see Elaine Showalter, "Feminist Criticism in the Wilderness"; and Sherry Ortner, "Is Female to Male as Nature is to Culture?"

5
~ Delia's Song ~

Lucha Corpi, a participant in the Chicano civil rights movement, has written novels involving issues and activities of the 1960s–1970s movement in which she makes it emphatically clear that personal lives and political issues are interwoven. *Delia's Song,* her first novel, is the story of a young woman named Delia Treviño. This character's painful stream of consciousness that frames the novel is a consequence of her brothers' deaths, one by a drug overdose and the other in Vietnam, and of her experience in the 1969 Berkeley strike by Chicano and other "Third World" students that was violently repressed by authorities.

Corpi has written two other novels that address significant events in the Chicano movement and the impact of these events on the central character of these novels, the detective Gloria Damasco. In *Eulogy for a Brown Angel,* Delia's 1992 novel, Gloria solves the mystery of a murdered Chicano child that she and her friend Luisa discover during the August 1970 National Chicano Moratorium against the Vietnam War in Los Angeles, at which police attacked both protesters who were angry over a police incident as well as peaceful families in Laguna Park. Her discovery of the child's body, his mouth stuffed with excrement, is so disturbing that Gloria momentarily leaves her body: "When I realized that the child was dead and his body so defiled, I felt a jolt moving from my chest to the back of my neck, then to my stomach. . . . I felt I was floating over the rooftops" (Corpi 1992: 18). Gloria's friend Luisa remarks, "You looked dead, too," which echoes Delia's deathlike appearance in *Delia's Song* (Corpi 19). This ability to float above the activities on the ground gives Gloria an overview of the moratorium events in the context of an oblivious city. She observes young and old people trying to help those overcome by the tear gas while police and sheriff's deputies are striking and arresting people. Gloria sees other areas of the economically and racially segregated city: "Brown and black men gazed on the world through the reeky mist of alcohol" while the rich Beverly Hills people shop at expensive stores and ride in their chauffeured limousines "towards their mansions, where their dark-skinned domestic staff tended to their every need" (Corpi 19). The moratorium occurred because the Vietnam War politicized the Chicano community with statistics indicating that the percentage of Chicano deaths in Vietnam was greater than their representation in the total population.

Between January 1961 and February 1967, although the Chicano population was officially 10 to 12 percent of the total population of the Southwest, the Chicano comprised 19.4 percent of those from that area who were killed. (Acuña 1972: 258)

In *Cactus Blood*, Corpi's 1995 novel, events of the 1973 farm workers strike and grape boycott intersect with the story of Carlota, a Mexican domestic servant, who is raped by her employer and poisoned by pesticides as she runs away through fields full of toxic crops. The novel opens with clairvoyant detective Gloria Damasco's premonition.

That's when I saw her. The woman. Naked. Her arms stretched up, tied to the fleshy leaves. Her legs together, bound to the stem. A slumping female Christ. . . . I know I will not rest until I learn for whose sins she was sacrificed. (Corpi 1995: n.p.)

This vision of a crucified woman refers to Remmi Stephens, a character who is pregnant and has been drugged and bound to a cactus when found by Gloria later in the novel. Yet the vision also signifies Corpi's concern with all the women who have suffered because of their race, class and gender, beginning with la Malinche, the native woman violated by Cortés, and continuing into the present day with women like Carlota, who are victims of rape, and farm workers, whose unborn babies can be damaged by pesticide poisoning. When Gloria and her colleague, Justin Escobar, listen to Carlota's taped story of her escape from Mexico in the trunk of a car, her rape at age fourteen by her employer and her subsequent suffering from pesticide poisoning, they both respond with visceral anger over the intimate details of one woman's oppression, which also reminds them of the collective oppression that inspired the Chicano activism of the 1960s and 1970s, especially the successful migrant farm workers union.

In the summer of 1970 the strike approached its fifth year. Many believed that the grape growers would never give in. . . . In June 1970, a group of growers agreed to sign contracts. They were followed by a majority of Coachella growers. Crates containing union grapes displayed the UFWOC flag with its eagle. (Acuña 1972: 182)

Cactus Blood is connected to Corpi's first novel, *Delia's Song,* because Delia is an invisible presence in this later novel. Though a fictional character, her poetry is quoted in the novel's epigraph and she is mentioned as one of the Chicana activists interviewed by Gloria's friend Luisa, who is collecting interviews for her book, *The Chicana Experience.* The character of Gloria, who has psychic abilities, discovers Justin reading an article by Foucault in an attempt to understand her psychic gift. This article, "Dreams, Imagination, and Existence," which suggests that dreams reveal the individual's potential for self-fulfillment, is also relevant to the nightmare-haunted Delia. In *Delia's Song,* she had numbed her heart against pain, resulting in a self-negation that leaves her feeling dead, or rather like Dracula, the "living dead." Her experience of feeling more dead than alive is a result both of her painful personal and cultural losses and her liminal position between Chicano and hegemonic culture. *Delia's Song* is the story of her recovery from this benumbed state of consciousness through her increased ability to find her voice and express her powerful emotions that emerged initially through nightmares.

In Delia's mind, the death of her brothers and her commitment to the Chicano movement are inextricably connected because she views their deaths as the result of social and economic oppression. She arrived at this realization when she encountered student activists at Berkeley who enabled her to understand the systemic oppression of Chicanos. "Before the emergence of the Chicano student movement in the late 1960s, intellectuals of Mexican descent were rare in U. S. public schools. In institutions of higher education, they were largely invisible" (Muñoz 1989: 127).

The history of Chicanos and the Mexican-United States border reveals the shifting state of the border, something that is virtually invisible in United States history lessons. Through the 1848 Treaty of Guadalupe Hidalgo, which ended the Mexican-American War, the United States expanded to include the previously Mexican areas of Texas, the Southwest and California. This resulted in an "occupied Mexico" within the borders of the United States, a population whose linguistic and cultural heritage was Mexican. "Beginning with the initial contacts with Mexicans on the frontier in the nineteenth century, Anglo-Americans exhibited contempt for the mixed-race Mexicans. During the process of annexation and conquest of what became the U. S. Southwest, this initial contempt turned to full-blown racism." (Rosales 1997: xxi)

As a result of this history, Gloria Anzaldúa describes the mestiza as one who has no homeland, yet belongs to all countries. The mestiza has to abandon rigid boundaries and habitual thought patterns in order to survive. Rather than engaging in an internalized border conflict between competing cultures, she must reconcile opposites through embracing flexibility and ambiguity. "At some point, on our way to a new consciousness, we will have to leave the opposite bank, the split between the two mortal combatants somehow healed so that we are on both shores at once and, at once, see through serpent and eagle eyes" (Anzaldúa 1987: 78).

At the opening of *Delia's Song*, Delia is still in the state of shock induced by personal losses and her experience of cultural conflict. Anzaldúa comments on the impact of this conflict, represented by the dichotomy between mental states labeled rational and irrational: "Like many Indians and Mexicans, I did not deem my psychic experiences real. . . . I allowed white rationality to tell me that the existence of the 'other world' was mere pagan superstition" (Anzaldúa 36). The reader first encounters Delia experiencing a nightmare. When she awakens from this nightmare, Delia prepares to attend a Day of the Dead party as St. Teresa, the Spanish mystic. Thus her dream states and interest in mysticism contend with the rational mentality required for her academic studies. "The other mode of consciousness facilitates images from the soul and the unconscious through dreams and the imagination. Its work is labeled 'fiction' " (Anzaldúa 37).

The conflict between the academic mentality and an indigenous worldview that validates the supernatural has induced Delia's *asustada* or *coatlicue* condition. Coatlicue, literally serpent woman, is an Aztec goddess of birth and death, signifying "a fusion of opposites: the eagle and the serpent, heaven and the underworld, life and death" (Anzaldúa 47). Gloria Anzaldúa describes her experience of being *coatlicue* or *asustada* as a refusal to recognize something about herself resulting in depression, which is called susto in Mexican culture, "the soul frightened out of the body" (Anzaldúa 48). This coatlicue state necessitates a voluntary descent into the underworld of one's consciousness, allowing oneself to let go of the need to understand rationally what must be experienced on a deeper level of the psyche, the level of dreams, powerful emotions, and psychological transformation. Once the fear of entering the darkness is overcome and the woman dares to enter the embrace of Coatlicue, "[s]uddenly the repressed energy rises, makes decisions, connects with conscious energy and a new life begins" (Anzaldúa 49).

Delia's state of depression resulting from repressed mourning also suggests la Llorona, a cultural symbol that Anzaldúa recognizes as instrumental in this process of healing border wounds. La Llorona is a descendant of the Aztec goddess Cihuacoatl. "Like la Llorona, Cihaucoatl howls and weeps in the night, screams as if demented. She brings mental depression and sorrow" (Anzaldúa 35–36). The tradition of la Llorona wailing for her lost children is an echo of the "mourning rites performed by women as they bid their sons, brothers and husbands good-bye" when they left for war (Anzaldúa 33). La Llorona may be searching for the lost parts of herself, which resembles Delia, who is trying to find an identity that doesn't require denying substantial parts of herself. Or perhaps she is crying for the losses of the colonial conquest and her lost children are "los Chicanos/mexicanos," which resonates with the themes of collective cultural and familial loss in all of Corpi's novels. In *Delia's Song*, the altars for the dead at her Aunt Marta's house and the Day of the Dead party given by her friend Mattie are Delia's reminders of the psychological need for mourning the dead and other losses.

Delia's Song is a narrative that integrates the personal experience of loss with the collective social and cultural losses of the Chicano people. The author, Lucha Corpi, bears witness to this social and political context as her novel documents the Third World Strike at Berkeley. Her main character, Delia, must evolve and grow in the context of these cultural and political circumstances of her life.

Mexican American students played a leading role in the organization of the Third World Liberation Front and the strike on the UC Berkeley campus [which] was aimed at exposing the university's lack of commitment to meeting the educational needs of third world people. (Muñoz 1989: 70)

They had envisioned a college with four separate departments, and they had been granted only one department with a meager budget to be divided among the ethnic groups. (Corpi 1989: 57–58)

Nine years later, Delia still suffers from threatening nightmares and is haunted by memories of the Berkeley violence. "Gas canisters Armed and ready they waited For us The damned The damned who dared Twisted faces of people in pain The pungent smell of blood and gas The sound of clubs against skulls arms legs" (Corpi 32). Delia, at the novel's opening scene, has not yet learned to release her repressed pain and express her true self. Though exhausted from completing her dissertation while supporting herself with a part-time job, she judges her accomplishments too harshly. Delia is so preoccupied with her obligations that she seems to have little capacity for enjoyment. As she begins to attire herself as the nun Teresa of Avila, her costume for the Day of the Dead party, Delia reflects on her life and the goals she had set for herself nine years earlier.

Delia had come to Berkeley in the fall of 1968 as a freshman full of plans—finish her degree, support her parents, do something for people in the barrio, marry and have a family. Nine years later, at age 28, she had achieved only one of her goals, a degree that seemed as useless as it had been hard to obtain. (Corpi 9)

As she walks to her car en route to the party, Delia notices a solitary rose and crosses the street for a closer look. Standing on the sidewalk in front of the rose, she is tormented by inner voices reminding her of incidents during the Berkeley strike, which ended with violent encounters between the students and the National Guard. Delia can't silence her inner chaos. Then she feels herself falling to the ground and slipping into unconsciousness. A voice asks, "Sister, are you all right?" and a man offers to help her. Delia notices the warmth of his touch because she has been feeling so cold. Although she sees the man only vaguely in the dim light, he seems familiar. When Delia asks him if his photo has appeared in the paper, the man laughs then says, "Yes, many people have seen my photo all over the world. . . . I am James Joyce, at least for tonight" (Corpi 12). Due to her extremely distraught condition, Delia wonders whether she really is crazy. She also recalls James Joyce's novel *Ulysses* and Molly Bloom's stream of consciousness: "And first I put my arms around him yes and drew him down to me so he could feel my breasts all perfume yes and his heart was going like mad and yes I said yes I will yes" (Corpi 12).

The man dressed as Joyce laughs about his masquerade and Delia also begins to laugh but rather hysterically. She responds, "You can't mean the writer. . . . The James Joyce. Don't you know you're dead? Dead!" (Corpi 13). "Joyce" is increasingly concerned about her behavior, finally offering to give her a ride home, which she refuses although she really wishes he wouldn't leave. After this strange encounter, Delia calms herself by admitting that the man she met was an imposter and wonders if he knows she too is an imposter of Saint Teresa.

While driving to the party, Delia worries about the possibility of hereditary madness in her family because of her Uncle Símon, whom people said had gone mad because of his "libertine ways." "Will I die with fireflies in my mouth too?" (Corpi 31). Then Delia remembers all the painful events of the past, especially her two dead brothers, and feels guilty because she is alive and well educated. Sebastian died of a drug overdose and her second brother, Ricardo, had gone into the Army to avoid Sebastian's fate but died on a battlefield.

When she arrives at Mattie's house, Delia notices the other guests at the party dressed as various historical and literary figures including Virginia Woolf, Sor Juana, Luis Valdez and Pancho Villa. Mattie greets Delia and mentions that George Sand is having a footbath because "Joyce bumped the table and that heavy bust of Beethoven fell on her foot" (Corpi 68). Delia is relieved to realize that the man she met was masquerading as Joyce for this party because this means that she hasn't been losing her mind. The guests dressed as Valdez, Murieta and Zapata remind Delia of the Mexican revolution and the Chicano movement and she feels overwhelming sadness over the failure of the strike/revolution and over the deaths of her brothers. Remembering all of her losses, Delia begins to cry.

If she started to cry, she would be crying a long time; for her two lost brothers, her parents whose three children had fallen victims of one kind of war or another, for all the people like her who believed they would make a difference and had gotten lost in some obscure corridor of academia. (Corpi 70)

The man she met earlier as James Joyce begins to comfort Delia. Recognizing his touch as he wipes her tears, Delia is moved by his tenderness. Their lovemaking in the garden recalls Delia's earlier reference to Molly Bloom when she first met Joyce on the sidewalk: "She buried her face in his neck and drew him to her, down to a bed of dewy grass in the mist" (Corpi 71). For both Delia and "James Joyce" their sexual encounter is bittersweet. Joyce remembers the painful experience of his wife's death, after which he felt like a "shadow in a spiritual wasteland" and during orgasm, Delia feels as if "her soul had escaped from her body through her gasping mouth, and she was dead" (Corpi 72). Later as he holds Delia and senses her painful tension, Joyce reflects that she is someone "who had lost a great deal, had perhaps mourned her losses too long" (Corpi 72). Roger/Joyce admits to her that he had felt guilty for desiring a nun but realized that his masquerade as James Joyce would make this acceptable.

The Day of the Dead party, especially the encounter there between Delia masquerading as Teresa of Avila and Roger masquerading as James Joyce, is the key event in *Delia's Song* because it constitutes a liminal space, a "betwixt and between" moment when normative behaviors are relaxed. According to Octavio Paz, at this liminal fiesta, order disappears and customary hierarchies of class and gender dissolve: "Regulations, habits and customs are violated. Respectable people put away the dignified expressions and conservative clothes that isolate them, dress up in gaudy colors, hide behind a mask and escape from themselves" (Paz 1961: 51). Due to her location between Anglo and Chicano cultures, Delia uneasily inhabits a permanent border zone in which she has not yet reconciled conflicting worldviews and obligations. At this party, she briefly enters a temporary liminal zone in which she can reconcile some conflicts and at last choose to make love simply because this is what she wants to do. Until this passionate encounter with Joyce, Delia has denied herself full participation in life because of her preoccupation with the dead and with her obligations as daughter and activist. Her friend's party functions as a transition between Delia's past, filled with loss, and the recovery of her ability to feel.

At the Day of the Dead party, Delia's masquerade as St. Teresa suggests the Spanish component of Mexico's mestizo culture but also a capacity for mystical consciousness that resembles Anzaldúa's notion of "la facultad," a psychic ability that balances what she calls "white rationality." James Joyce was an Irish writer who expressed the complexities of the colonized consciousness and posited an alternative more fluid consciousness in his novels *Ulysses* and *Finnegan's Wake*. Because the Day of the Dead, or All Soul's Day, is a traditional Mexican and Catholic holy day for the remembrance of those who have died, it is appropriate that Delia and James Joyce/Roger would feel their losses more acutely at this time.

In Mexican tradition the worlds of the living and of the dead intermingle during the Day of the Dead festival when people visit their relatives' graves and make altars with offerings of food and flowers to the dead. The Spanish brought the custom of making offerings to the dead with them when they conquered the New World, and this custom merged with Aztec rituals of death. "The European customs of making food-offerings and feasting with the dead found fertile ground in Mexico where superficially similar ceremonies were an important aspect of pre-Hispanic religious ritual" (Carmichael 1992: 15). Aztec poetry recognized the ephemeral nature of life and *flor y canto* (flower and song) was the "ancient Aztec metaphor for poetry" (Sayer 1990: 13). Both Irish and Mexican Catholicism retain pre-Christian elements such as observing All Soul's Day, *Samhain* in Celtic culture or *Día de los Muertos* in Mexican culture, a time when the souls of the dead return to visit the living or at least when the living remember their dead relatives.

"Chicanos can't afford not to be ruled by their ghosts. We're like ants who carry their dead on their shoulders" (Corpi 1989: 76). Once when Delia visited her Aunt Marta in Monterey, they made an altar of the dead. Their altar had candy skulls and bread for the dead and included pictures of

John F. Kennedy and Pope John XXIII next to a medal of the Sacred Heart. Her aunt had also included embroideries of two folk heroes, Tiburcio Vásquez and Joaquín Murieta on either side of the Virgen de Guadalupe. When Delia begins to write her story and mourn the death of her brothers and the death of her ideals for the Chicano student movement, she is actually creating her altars for the dead people and dead dreams in her life.

When Joyce first encountered Delia collapsing on the sidewalk, she appeared to be a nun kneeling at a rosebush in prayer. "The solitary rose in November Collective memory of spring on a bare limb" (Corpi 10). In fact Delia's mind is besieged with fragments of painful memories and fragments of prayer remembered from childhood, interwoven with appeals to her parents, "Mother Mother. . . . Papa hold me Hold me" (Corpi 11). This solitary rosebush is a symbol of the transience of life associated with observations of the Day of the Dead, when graves are covered with flowers and food offerings. "Our popular images always poke fun at life affirming the nothingness and insignificance of human existence. We decorate our houses with death's heads, we eat bread in the shape of bones on the Day of the Dead" (Paz 1961: 59). In this instance, the solitary rosebush evokes the roses on the altar of the dead that Delia made with Marta and also reminds us that Delia is the only child remaining in her family.

Delia is haunted by memories that take over her dreams, creating violent nightmares composed of fragments from the past. Even her waking consciousness is haunted by these painful memories involving the loss of her brothers but also a multiplicity of other losses, including the loss of her mother's love, the loss of her hopes and dreams for the Chicano movement at Berkeley and especially perhaps the loss of her childhood.[1] "I've lost something essential. Maybe some innocence, faith" (Corpi 1989: 6). This theme of loss and mourning is also important in Julia O'Faolain's *No Country for Young Men*. The nun Judith and her great-niece are survivors who have lost family members and are aware of the tremendous losses in the last century of Irish history, the famine of 1845–1852, when at least a million people died and another two million or more emigrated; the war of independence with Britain; and the civil war that followed.

Significantly, by being dressed as the Irish author James Joyce, Delia's phantom lover suggests a connection of two peoples that have been colonized and suffered personal and collective losses. The ghostly influence of James Joyce combines with her painful memories to haunt Delia and finally inspires her to write her story. Delia doesn't meet Roger, "Joyce," again until the end of the novel but becomes obsessed with him or rather with what he symbolizes for her. James Joyce's novels describe the psychological implications of colonialism and the nightmare of Irish history. Some of the colonial issues that pervade Joyce's work are also significant in Delia's consciousness. For example, she is tormented by violent nightmares in which her tongue is cut until she finally realizes, "Victim and victimizer. . . . I sliced my own tongue" (Corpi 145). Bloom in *Ulysses* experiences a nightmare sequence in which a dominatrix in a brothel whips him. The manner in which colonialism makes the victim become his or her own victimizer is recognized by both Joyce and by Corpi as are the masks or roles that are imposed on colonized people.

The Mexican, whether young or old, criollo or mestizo, general or laborer or lawyer, seems to me to be a person who shuts himself away to protect himself: his face is a mask and so is his smile. (Paz 1961: 29)

Delia and Julio reject these imposed masks when they discuss changing the name of MASC (Mexican American Student Confederation) to MECHA (Movimiento Estudiantil Chicano de Aztlán): "No more MASC. No more masks. We are, who we are" (Corpi 1989: 24). Her gradual realization of oppression, the example of her father's humiliation in his job and the tragedy of her brothers' deaths shape Delia's childhood. Her childhood is also sad because her mother, grief stricken over the deaths of her sons, withdraws from Delia, who feels obligated to fulfill her parents' dreams for their sons in order to compensate them for these losses.

Due to her experience of multiple oppressions, race, class and gender, it is difficult for a woman such as Delia to obtain a sense of self, the autonomy to choose what she wants rather than what others want for her, when she is pressured by familial and political expectations. Since Delia's oppression is both external and internalized, she struggles to change the society she inhabits as well as change herself by resisting the internalized scripts that have been directing her life. At first there are the expectations of her parents that one of their children will escape poverty and achieve respect in the Anglo world. Then there are the expectations of MASC, later MECHA, that impose political obligations depriving Delia of simply enjoying her life: "La raza La causa But not love Or eroticism for that matter" (Corpi 129). Yet Delia is not only denied the pleasure of love or sexuality but she is also denied the pleasure of doing something simply because she wants to do it. Even the writing of her dissertation seems a burden that prevents her from writing poetry. Finally, at the Day of the Dead party, Delia is able to express her true self while masquerading as Teresa of Avila.

Take those two terms mask and masquerade, which reappear conspicuously and are both meant, worn as they are, as weapons of survival. But the former is there to represent a burden, imposed, constraining the expression of one's real identity; the latter is flaunted, or . . . at least put on like a new dress which, even when required, does give some pleasure to the wearer. (De Lauretis 1986: 17)

Throughout the novel, Delia has a recurring fantasy about her sexual encounter with "James Joyce," which represents the first time she has actively chosen something for herself rather than passively accepting others' expectations. The actual James Joyce challenged Irish stereotypes of women with his Molly Bloom character, a sexually active woman in *Ulysses*, just as Corpi, through her character Delia initiating the sexual encounter with "James Joyce," challenges stereotypes of Chicana women. In Mexican history, la Malinche has been portrayed as the woman who betrayed her people by becoming Cortés's mistress, thus "[t]he potential accusation of 'traitor' or 'vendida' is what hangs above the heads and beats in the hearts of most Chicanas seeking to develop our own autonomous sense of ourselves, particularly through sexuality" (Moraga 1983:103). Irish patriots such as Patrick Pearse, who wrote poems glorifying motherhood and Mother Ireland, established a similar pattern of female purity. James Joyce especially rejected the national ideology of "Irish purity which linked a wholly false notion of the Gael to the equally false notion of the sexually and racially pure Irish person-to be more specific, the pure Irish woman" (MacCabe, quoted in Maddox 1988: 381)

The women in *No Country for Young Men* struggle with accepting their sexuality, which is in conflict with these images of the pure Irish woman. Judith remembers a priest who breaks down and cries as he tells the young schoolgirls how he is restored by their innocence: "How can I ever tell you the joy it brings to my heart to see innocence abloom today in this ancient, holy and sacred land?"(O'Faolain 1980: 301). Years later, women like her great niece Gráinne are more accepting of their sexuality. The literary characters Delia and Gráinne are indebted to the literary precedent of James Joyce's Molly with her sexually explicit interior monologue.

Mexican-American culture like Irish culture is strongly influenced by Catholicism, which played a role in the Spanish colonization of indigenous peoples in the New World. A knowledge of Catholicism and the role played in Catholic culture by confession and guilt contributes to an understanding of Delia. As Stephen Daedalus explores the voyeuristic aspects of the confessional and the guilt associated with his Catholic conditioning in *Portrait of the Artist as a Young Man*, Delia also explores her inexplicable feeling of guilt and wonders, "Why am I always asking for forgiveness What have I done but be beaten and get up every time Is that my sin" (Corpi 1989: 163). When Delia tells her friend Mattie that she wants Jeff to know everything including the event with "Joyce," Mattie tells her, "The Catholic Church did quite a job on you. This need to confess" (Corpi 190).

Dervorgilla is an Irish parallel to la Malinche. In *No Country for Young Men*, the young Judith, who eventually becomes a nun, remembers a history lesson that the frail morals of a woman were first responsible for bringing the English to Ireland in 1169—so "[w]omen bore inherited guilt" (O'Faolain 1980: 34). The woman was Dervorgilla, whose affair caused fighting between her husband and lover. When her lover Diarmuid fled to England for help, this began the English occupation of Ireland (Weekes 1990: 184). In the case of Irish, Mexican or Mexican-American women like Delia, the Catholic message of guilt is overlaid with the guilt of conquest displaced on women who are associated with the betrayal of la Malinche or Dervorgilla.

La Malinche was given to Cortés as his translator because she knew Maya and Nahautl. She became Cortés's mistress and bore his child. When Cortés's Spanish wife came to Mexico, he married la Malinche to one of his soldiers. Octavio Paz states that the Mexican people have not forgiven la Malinche for betraying her Indian civilization by assisting Cortés and becoming his mistress. For Paz she is a symbol of betrayal because she allowed herself to be penetrated by the Spanish male. The expression *la chingada* or *hijo de la chingada* (son of the violated one) is used to demean all women and mothers, not only la Malinche. "If the Chingada is a representation of the violated Mother, it is appropriate to associate her with the Conquest, which was also a violation, not only in the historical sense but also in the very flesh of Indian women. The symbol of this violation is doña Malinche, the mistress of Cortés" (Paz 1961: 86). In reality, la Malinche was both slave and skillful translator. She has been redeemed recently by various female critics who view her as a talented woman betrayed by her family and Cortés and silenced by a history that does not tell of la Malinche's response to these events. La Malinche was a commodified woman whose use in the "transfer of females through which Malintzin became Doña Marina" signified the "military exchange of power from the Indian states to the Spanish foreigners" (Cypess 1991: 81). In retrospect, it is possible to view la Malinche as an intelligent colonized woman masquerading as translator and lover to Cortés in order to render the inevitable conquest less brutal for her people.

In her Marina poems, Corpi portrays la Malinche rather as a victim of betrayal, someone who was sold by her family then "*negada y desecrada*" by

Cortés then blamed for her desecration by her son who calls her "*la chingada*" (Sánchez 1985: 184). This reverses the traditional view articulated by Octavio Paz in his analysis of the Mexican psyche. In the patriarchal, colonial, "binary Manichean system of thought Guadeloupe's transcendentalizing power, silence and maternal self-sacrifice are the positive, contrasting attributes to those of a woman who speaks as a sexual being and independently of her maternal role . . . as Malintzin did" (Alarcón 1989: 62). Corpi's four poems about Marina reinterpret her "not as a woman who betrayed [se vendió], but as a woman who was betrayed [fué vendida] by husband, lover, and son. Implicitly, she was also betrayed by family, culture, and country" (Sánchez 1985: 184). By revising representations of la Malinche, Chicanas revise the image of motherhood and of women.

In Corpi's Marina poems, the stanza of Marina Virgen follows the stanza of Marina Madre thus suggesting that virginity is not so much a physical condition. In fact in this poem virginity is associated with Marina's identification with the crucified Christ as "mujer sufrida, or the long-suffering Mexican woman" (Sánchez 191). Delia and her mother are stoically suffering women in the sense described by Paz. "Through suffering, our women become like our men: invulnerable, impassive, and stoic" (Paz 1961: 39). However, in addition to the Christian images in these Marina poems, there is also a pre-Columbian subtext. Like Delia of *Delia's Song* and Gloria of *Cactus Blood*, Corpi's Marina has ancestral mystical, poetic and psychic qualities. "Corpi portrays Marina as a mystic, steeped in tradition, that is, she was the holder of ancient ritual and knowledge, a knowledge that does not disappear because you are silent" (Rebolledo 1995: 67).

La Malinche's historical importance as translator symbolizes Chicana writers' mediation between languages and cultures. This relates to Delia's struggle with silence and language because colonialism silences the colonized and imposes the language of the colonizer. Sometimes Delia speaks in Spanish or Chicano Spanish and other times in English. She is as caught between these languages as Irish authors like Joyce were caught between Irish and English. Joyce opted for a third alternative finally in *Finnegan's Wake*, when he creates a new language of English-based neologisms using the rhythm of Irish. Joyce used various linguistic modes in his writing and thus "exploited the complex linguistic situation in Ireland to serve his goal. . . . The English spoken by the mass of the Irish people and partly recorded in the works of these writers, was oral-formulaic in its compositional principle and closely related to Irish" (Deane 1990: 42). For Irish authors then as now, the language question signifies much more than merely the choice of language in which to communicate but more deeply the profound psychological conflict for those living in a condition of colonialism, when the predominant language of expression is the colonizer's language and when the native language embodies a culture that has been disrupted by the colonization process.

The language in which we are speaking is his before it is mine. How different are the words home, Christ, ale, master, on his lips and on mine! I cannot speak or write these words without unrest of spirit. His language, so familiar and so foreign, will always be for me an acquired speech. (Joyce 1977: 189)

[Delia] began telling it in Spanish, which she always spoke with her aunt, but as she related the episode about her near-accident and her fear of being mad, she switched to English. (Corpi 1989: 99)

The issue of colonialist repression of indigenous languages is aligned with other forms of censorship. James Joyce's work was censored in his native Ireland because of its explicit sexuality but one wonders if it was not also due to his often harsh criticism of Irish subservience to British and Catholic authority. St. Teresa was not explicitly censored yet the fact that she was commanded by her confessor to write must certainly have made her writing a less than spontaneous act of self-expression. Delia has a nightmare in which some man is slicing her tongue. What frightens her most is that she doesn't resist her loss of tongue, "[t]he very instrument of voice" (Corpi 127). Eventually, Delia understands this nightmare as a form of self-censorship realizing that she has internalized the censor and is silencing herself. This motif of the tongue also suggests la Malinche, who was referred to by Spanish chroniclers as "la lengua ('the tongue')" because of her facility with languages (Sánchez 1985: 187). Women like la Malinche and the women authors at the Day of the Dead party like Sor Juana, St. Teresa and Delmira Augustini had potentially dangerous tongues that necessitated patriarchal control and silencing.

Those who have turned their tongues 10,000 times seven times before not speaking are either dead from it or more familiar with their tongues and their mouths than anyone else. (Cixous 1980: 257)

Delia's choice of St. Teresa for her masquerade has multiple meanings in the novel as does Roger's masquerade as Joyce. While she claims that the choice was influenced by her interest in St. Teresa's passionate quest for love, her choice also suggests an identification with the problems of self-expression for a woman mystic who has to rely on patriarchal language. St. Teresa has been much admired for her courage in writing about her mystical experience during a time when she could have been punished by the Spanish Inquisition. Yet it is believed that St. Teresa escaped the Inquisition "not only because she had influential friends, but because she wrote" in obedience to the command of her confessors (Kamboureli 1989: 58).

Teresa used erotic imagery to write about her mystical experience, which is not easily described by language. "With this [spear] he seemed to pierce my heart several times so that it penetrated to my entrails. . . . The pain was so sharp that it made me utter several moans; and so excessive was the sweetness caused me by this intense pain that one can never wish to lose it" (Teresa, quoted in Kamboureli 1989: 55). Delia imitates St. Teresa when she chooses the language of intimacy to write herself out of her emotional crisis/nightmare, a language that would have been unsuitable to the dissertation she has just completed. This erotic mysticism of Teresa implies that sexuality and spirituality are not binary opposites and that women need not be polarized as either virginal saints or sexual creatures. "By 1900 writers and painters, scientists and critics, the learned and the modish alike had been indoctrinated to regard all women who no longer conformed to the image of the household nun as vicious, bestial creatures, representative of a pre-evolutionary, instinctual past" (Dijkstra 1986: 324–25). Delia's masquerade as an erotic nun deconstructs these binary stereotypes.

Teresa's use of the confessional genre offers another interesting parallel to Delia's writing. Both women subvert this genre by using it to justify themselves rather than to ask forgiveness: "Maybe she was grasping at straws, hoping to find a way to get herself out of spiritual deprivation, but a voice inside kept assuring her that writing would help her restore proper order to a world that had collapsed around her" (Corpi 1989: 78). Any number of Teresa's beliefs could have been considered heretical by the Inquisition because Teresa's experience of prayer as communion with the divine is mystical and "the mystic's ineffable, antiintellectual experience of the divine is, ultimately, nonhierarchical and antiinstitutional" (Weber 1990: 35). Since St. Teresa had been suspected of being involved with the devil rather than with God, her relationship with her confessors and her writing under their direction was a means of self-defense during the Inquisition. Teresa in fact advises women to be careful in their choice of confessors and maintain secrecy if necessary because her confessors talked about her to each other: "They have done me great harm, divulging things which should have been kept secret for they are not meant for everyone to know"

(Teresa, quoted in Kamboureli 1989: 60). Marie Kramb describes Teresa's style as a "careful rhetoric of self-depreciation which involves several strategic moves: an affected modesty . . . a pose of contrition . . . and a narrative voice which registers as orthodox and exemplary actions which actually entail protest" (Kramb 1992: 111–12).

The presence of Sor Juana Inés de la Cruz, a nun who lived in seventeenth-century Mexico, as another party guest suggests parallels between Teresa and Sor Juana as well as between the two nuns and Delia. Teresa and Sor Juana both wrote passionately about love. Whereas for Teresa this was a mystical love of God, for Sor Juana her passion was primarily intellectual and her love lyrics describe a more secular relationship. Both Sor Juana and Teresa had separations from their mothers at an early age. Teresa's mother died when she was fourteen. "When I began to understand what I had lost, I went, afflicted, before an image of our Lady and besought her with many tears to be my mother" (Knuth 1994: 133). Sor Juana's brilliance was discovered at an early age and her mother sent her to live with a married sister when Juana was only ten. Though ostensibly this action was motivated by concern for her, it may also have been convenient for her mother, who had entered into a love affair.

Sor Juana could serve as a prototype for Delia because she was an intelligent and educated woman at a time when this was uncommon. Both Sor Juana and Delia have rejected feminine cultural stereotypes by developing their intellects. "In writings such as her 'Respuesta' and the 'Autodefensa espiritual' (Spiritual Self-Defense), Sor Juana militantly defends a woman's right to education and, by implication, participation in the male order" (Merrim 1991: 22). Sor Juana, like Delia and Teresa, is a woman mourning both personal loss and her loneliness in a world unreceptive to so brilliant a woman. Her love poems resemble Delia's obsession with the phantom lover James Joyce and have been interpreted as expressions of unrequited love.

Sor Juana's male characters . . . are invariably shadows, incorporeal ideas; "fantastic" phantoms—in sum, absences recreated in the solitude of unreciprocated love. (Merrim 19)

As did St. Teresa with love of God, Sor Juana used love of learning as a "poetic theme and invested it with the fateful intensity of erotic love" (Merrim 19). Similarly, Delia's attachment to the memory of her sexual encounter with Joyce becomes transformed into a love affair with her writing. Hélène Cixous describes the desire to write as erotic. In fact the passion of writing controls and ravishes the writer: "First I am touched, caressed, wounded; then I try to discover the secret of this touch to extend it, celebrate it, and transform it into another caress" (Cixous 1991: 45). In effect, by loving God, as in the case of Teresa, or a phantom lover, as in the case of Delia and Sor Juana, these women maintain their virginity, not primarily in the physical sense but rather in the sense of a woman who is autonomous.

According to Octavio Paz, Sor Juana's "presumptuous tone" in her defense of women's rights in the "Respuesta a Sor Filotea de la Cruz" alienated the Bishop of Puebla and her confessor and caused them to withdraw their support thus requiring her to renounce her pursuit of secular knowledge. Yet the "Respuesta" adopts a rhetorical code acceptable for women whereas the "Autodefensa Espiritual," a personal letter to her confessor written ten years before the "Respuesta," uses quite different language: "Rather than the unctuous rhetoric of subordination, here we find assertive and biting invective with no subterfuges. . . . Sor Juana's true voice? A Sor Juana with no mask?" (Merrim 1991: 28). Not only is Delia masquerading as Teresa, but contemporary views of Teresa and Sor Juana demonstrate that both nuns strategically wore discursive "masks" of humility and subordination that concealed women considerably more complex than their facades.[2]

Delmira Agustini, one of the other "guests" attending the Day of the Dead party, was an early nineteenth-century Uruguayan poet who also created fantasy lovers in her poetry. One of her poems is entitled "Boca a boca" (mouth to mouth) and has this line, "Vampiro vuelto mariposa al día" [the vampire turns into a butterfly by day] (Norat 1990: 154). Other poems describe desire as cannibalism and masochism. The following lines are from a poem entitled "El vampiro."

> ?Por qué fue tu vampiro de amargura? . . .
> Soy flor o estirpe de una especie oscura
> Que come llagas y que bebe el llanto (Norat 159)

> Why were you a vampire of bitterness?
> I am a flower or the lineage of an obscure species
> That eats sores and that drinks tears. [my translation]

Gisela Norat, in her article on Agustini, "Vampirismo, sadismo y masoquismo en la poesia de Delmira Agustini," suggests that the poet's obsession with this dark side of desire reflects her resentment of maternal oppression of daughters in obedience to patriarchal law.

Por qué la mujer incuba tanta animosidad contra la madre? La respuesta parece radicar en que la madre es la primera figura autoritaria y, por lo tanto, para la niña

ésta representa prohibiciones de todo tipo. En lo sexual la madre le prohíbe la
masturbación y la regaña por otras expresiones de carácter sexual. (Norat 160)

Why does the woman incubate such animosity against her mother? The answer
appears to lie in that the mother is the primary authority figure and therefore for
the daughter represents prohibitions of every type. In sexual matters her mother
prohibits masturbation and scolds her for other expressions of a sexual nature.

Citing Adrienne Rich in *Of Woman Born* that the mother is an en-
forcer of the patriarchy, Norat sees Agustini as resentful of this repressive socialization at the hands of her mother, so that she views maternal
love as vampirism, sucking the passion out of children, especially
daughters. Agustini had to conceal her creative and sexual passion because it was not acceptable in an Uruguayan woman of that era. Thus
another aspect of the vampire motif is that a powerful woman was perceived as dangerous like the seductive vampire. Therefore she must
wear a mask of subservience appearing as a butterfly by day, "vampiro
vuelto mariposa al día" (Norat 154). In the 1960s and 1970s, when
Delia's Song occurs, it was still generally true of the Chicano family that
"[w]omen are particularly ostracized socially for being sexually active
outside of marriage, and more than that, are stigmatized if they are a
single parent" (Garcia-Bahne 1977: 37). Delia at the Day of the Dead
party sees herself in the mirror as "Dracula the undead," reflecting her
inner conflict over gender and cultural roles but also suggesting her repressed passion, which will soon be expressed with James Joyce/Roger
(Corpi 1989: 69).

Los versos donde surge el vampirismo son una reacción al escesivo cariño materno
que, llevado al extremo, desangra la propia vida de la hija. . . . Pero en el fondo de
los versos sádicos hay una venganza contra la madre por someter a la hija a las
injusticias del sistema patriarcal. (Norat 1990: 163)

The verses from which vampirism surges are a reaction to the excessive maternal
care that, carried to the extreme, drains the very life from the daughter. . . . But at
the bottom of these sadistic verses there is a vengeance against the mother for
submitting her daughter to the injustices of the patriarchal system.

The passion that is repressed by the patriarchal mother is not only eroticism, as signified by the sexual encounter of St. Teresa/Delia and James
Joyce/Roger, but also a passion for life which opposes the patriarchal oppression that has drawn Delia's brothers into death through the Vietnam
War or through the machismo life of the barrio. When she becomes involved in the student movement, Delia learns from Samuel about the social

factors contributing to this outcome for her brothers. " 'White supremacy. Colonialism. Whatever we want to call it. It spells racism, oppression. No choices.' He looked at Delia hanging onto every word. 'Your brothers were both victims of it' " (Corpi 1989: 89).

Although Delia begins to understand the web of systematized circumstances—colonialism, poverty and war—that destroys the oppressed, she still blames her parents, especially her mother, for enforcing the patriarchy and not protecting her sons. "My mother could have done something. At least tell Ricardo not to enlist. . . . She's to blame" (Corpi 90). In fact Delia resents her mother not only for not preventing her brother's death but also because she believes her mother rejected her for not being male. Delia thinks that her mother preferred her sons and is disappointed to be left with only a daughter. "Why can't you love me Mother Why I'm not much but I'm all you've got All you've got" (Corpi 33). Though her friend Mattie tries to tell her that she's not responsible for her brothers' deaths or her father's weakness, Delia holds unrealistically demanding expectations for herself, hoping to win her mother's approval.

In daily life, Agustini seemed a docile, obedient daughter who conformed and married a conventional man, but at night she wrote intensely erotic poetry. Eventually, Agustini was unable to repress this passionate side, leaving her husband after only two months and beginning a liaison with a fellow poet. Her husband could not accept this rejection and in 1914 he shot Agustini and then killed himself. Agustini had consigned her passionate rebellious side to her poetry. When she tried to unite her two roles in real life, "[t]he men of her time were not prepared for this new woman" (Fox-Lockert 1987: 41). Sor Juana was silenced by her Church, but Delmira Agustini was silenced by her husband's revolver.

Delmira's mask of docile daughter is like Delia's mask of dutiful daughter and dutiful political activist. Some masks are cultural and others gendered. When Delia first hears the name of the Chicano students group, MASC, it sounds like "mask." Chicano/as have worn masks to please Anglo society and Delia has worn masks to please her parents and men. At a previous Day of the Dead party, whose theme was to dress as anything to do with death, Delia dressed as Camille in La Traviata, the courtesan dying of consumption. "Living dead Loving dead" (Corpi 1989:63). At that party she met Fernando, with whom she has an emotionally abusive relationship. After awhile Fernando controls Delia with his cruelty until her nightmares become worse. "There was something in her, however, which had not allowed her to carry out her death wish," and when Fernando's abuse became physical and he hit her, Delia picked up a dictionary of the Spanish language and struck him.

In Delia's nightmare at the novel's opening scene, the interpersonal violence of her relationship with her controlling ex-boyfriend, Fernando, is combined with the violent repression of the student strike at Berkeley. She invokes the name of the Father in this dream as she tries to pray the "Our Father." This dream later erupts into her consciousness on her way to the Day of the Dead party, and she tries to drown out the tormenting inner voices with this prayer again but finds herself calling for her mother and father. Despite this appeal to them, Delia is aware that her parents, themselves victims of systemic oppression, are unable to protect her. Her father is forced to obey a stereotype of a humble and submissive Chicano in order to keep his job and her mother cannot teach her sons to resist the patriarchy nor can she value her daughter as an autonomous subject.

As a survivor of the political battles of the Berkeley Chicano student movement of the late 1960s, Delia knows that the temptation to retreat to a private world of romanticism is unrealistic. The pain of social and economic oppression has had such an impact on Delia, her family and friends that she knows there is no escaping it through romantic love. The complex problems of gender, race and class will accompany her into any love affair, marriage or career she might enter. Thus her efforts to achieve self-realization cannot be separated from her awareness of the historical oppression of Mexican Americans and the need to continue working for social change. At the same time, Delia recognizes the complexity of racism, noting that Professor Ruvalcaba, though "Brown like [Delia]," used the expression "You Chicanos" (Corpi 1989: 102).

Delia's Song challenges stereotypical notions of the Mexican-American family and expectations for Chicanas. "Most often, the father takes on an authoritarian, dominant role as a result of wanting to be an effective parent," and "[t]he family and marriage get viewed as the only vehicles by which a woman can validly find expression of her values regarding her sexuality, thus binding her to childbearing and maintenance of family cohesiveness" (Garcia-Bahne 1977: 36–37). In this novel, Delia's father is more vulnerable than her detached mother is and he is the one who actually breaks down and cries with her when his son dies. Garcia-Bahne criticizes the view that cultural factors are solely responsible for the Chicano family's overvaluation of the male, its characteristics of "paternalism, authoritarianism, low levels of aspiration, fatalism, female passivity and male domination" (Garcia-Bahne 40). She argues that the Chicano family's low-income status as a result of economic oppression has fostered many of these characteristics because the cohesive family becomes the one place where the "man is not powerless, as in his job, and can in fact exercise some dominance, i.e., over his wife and children" (Garcia-Bahne 38).

Delia resists a female identity limited to marriage by obtaining her Ph.D. and by ending the abusive relationship with Fernando. Yet after she finished her dissertation, Delia wandered around the campus aimlessly. Her goal of fulfilling her family's expectations is accomplished and she still doesn't know who she is. Upon seeing her reflection in the lake, she doesn't even recognize herself because it is a false self: "Not wanting to believe it was her own, she looked over her shoulder expecting someone else to be standing beside her" (Corpi 1989: 65). When Delia arrives at the Day of the Dead party after her collapse, Mattie tells her she looks like a worn-out courtesan. Delia goes to the mirror and sees that her rouge is gone and her eye make-up had run, leaving dark rings around her eyes. She thinks that she looks "more like Dracula the undead" than either a courtesan or St. Teresa. Delia is asustada which, as described earlier by Anzaldúa, is an avoidance of painful authenticity. Wearing her multiple masks of a woman negotiating the complex oppressions of race, class and gender, Delia's authentic self is buried under this weighty burden.

In Mexico, people are recognized as suffering from a folk illness, *susto*, whose symptoms resemble Delia's condition of generalized anxiety, fatigue, sleep disturbance and loss of consciousness. A study of this condition has found that it occurs more frequently among women because they are "emotionally taxed more heavily than their male counterparts" (Rubel 1984: 78). Susto is usually not the result of a sudden shock but rather of cumulative debilitation "resulting from social problems with which the victim was unable to cope" (Rubel 13–14). The stress is often caused by the individual's perception that he or she is unable to successfully fulfill their social role or masks, a role that perhaps in an atmosphere of the cultural and social crisis of colonization and industrialization is really beyond anyone's capacity to fill. Susto explains the individual's condition as the result of having lost soul or some of their vital essence, which resembles Delia's repeated references to feeling dead or feeling her soul escape.

Suffering susto, being asustado, is based on people's understanding that an individual is composed of a body and an immaterial substance, an essence, that may become detached from the body and either wander freely or become a captive of supernatural forces. (Rubel 8)

When Delia masquerades as St. Teresa, this masquerade is an empowering rejection of her previous masks and a new relationship with the ghosts of her personal and cultural history. The Day of the Dead party and her meeting with Joyce awakens her from being *asustada*. Delia's masquerade as a nun subverts this image of virginal femininity by her engaging in an erotic encounter. Yet after they make love and Joyce refers to her as Teresa, Delia wonders, "Why must I always impersonate someone?" (Corpi 1989: 72). In her spontaneous act of love with James Joyce, Delia expresses the repressed emotions and passions that lie buried beneath her facade, or mask. · After this awakening, Delia goes to stay with her Aunt Marta and there meets her old friend Jeff from her early days in Berkeley. After they become lovers, Jeff reflects how "[u]nder the poised and demure face and manner lived a woman haunted by fury and sorrow, a woman he loved and yet did not know well" (Corpi 128). No one, including her friend Jeff, can know Delia until she accepts herself. As their relationship develops, Delia realizes that she has generally chosen relationships that she knows will not require a permanent commitment and also that she has never said I love you to anyone, not even to Jeff.

Delia remembers "James Joyce" and how once with him she expressed her desire. "Only once, I did what I wanted to do" (Corpi 141). Delia's masks conceal repressed desire as well as repressed pain. Her disguise as the nun St. Teresa is a masquerade of femininity that conceals her erotic and intellectual identity and temporarily removes her from the marketplace of male desire. The events of her life allowed her to attend college and reverse the traditional role of a Mexican American daughter. At Berkeley, Delia takes a course with Mattie, a professor who becomes a friend. Mattie is a member of the Socialist Alliance for Progress, who has helped to organize a worker's strike and later goes to Central America to help publicize the truth about the revolutionary efforts to change conditions in Guatemala, Honduras, El Salvador and Nicaragua.

Once, early in Delia's relationship with Mattie, the latter was encouraging the students in her class to speak frankly. Delia however was conditioned to accept authority and hesitated to speak in class. Mattie tries to elicit Delia's opinion by asking, "Don't you think that everyone has a right to a safe environment and to an equal share in the benefits of his labor?" (Corpi 17). Delia wondered if this was really true, feeling that her family did not share in the so-called American dream and that she was an exception only because an Anglo nun in high school had encouraged her. Mattie suggests that Delia meet Samuel Corona, a graduate student in sociology, for advice in writing about the socioeconomic status of Mexican Americans. When Delia realizes how little information is available on this topic in 1968, she is shocked by the invisibility of Mexican Americans in the United

States and understands the necessity for the Chicano movement. Delia also learns about the university's involvement in agricultural research to benefit the growers but not the farm workers, who are mainly Mexican Americans. Samuel explains, "It's the power elite. The University has no trouble justifying doing research for agri-business, but . . . U.C. is definitely not on our side" (Corpi 25).

The family stories that Delia hears from Aunt Marta are as significant for her as knowledge of these revolutionary ideas. Marta's stories are about accomplishments, losses and survival in Delia's family, and they are therefore stories that help her understand conditions in her family and the transgenerational repression of pain that made it difficult for her family to heal the loss of her brothers. "Asuncion Aguirre Cadena, your great grandmother, was a skilled silversmith. . . . I can close my eyes and still remember the rhythmic murmur of her voice at night telling us stories and legends of long ago" (Corpi 84). From Marta, Delia learns of Asuncion's brother Símon, who went mad and died with his mouth full of fireflies. She hears about her grandparents, her grandfather who was a grain trader and her grandmother who was a curandera. Marta tells Delia about the earthquake that killed most of the family. Marta, Delia's father and Uncle Chino were the only survivors and they decided to go to California. Delia's mother met the man who became her husband shortly after she was left alone, when her mother was killed by a car while crossing the street. "For seven summers Delia had lived in a bountiful place where music, legend and family history were consumed every day like food to keep alive and healthy" (Corpi 93). In Marta's home, Delia began to understand that this is what people meant by the dynamics of culture. "As I have told you their story, so must you tell it to your children and their children" (Corpi 86).

The autobiographical novel that Delia writes and shares with Aunt Marta is a story of the Chicano student movement's resistance to oppression but, just as importantly, it's a personal story that speaks of her family's unspoken pain and of Delia's refusal to choose between autonomy and relationship. She will risk losing Jeff rather than deny herself, although she hopes that he will still love her as an autonomous woman. Delia knows that she must show Jeff what she has written about her life and risk deromanticizing their relationship because "I can't go on telling half-truths to myself and to those I love" (Corpi 190). The obsession with Roger as "James Joyce" suggests Delia's symbolic relationship with the real James Joyce, who inspires her to recover from her attack of susto by writing the truth of her life as a Chicana. Of all the female characters in these four novels that are struggling to find a personal voice in the midst of overwhelming historical pressures and personal pain, Delia manages to create an identity through her writing that encompasses both her personal desires and her commitment to social change. While she continues to realize that the political action of the Chicano student movement and strike were essential to gaining access to higher education for Chicanos, she now realizes that this is not enough if mothers still allow their children to die in war or from drugs. Thus she hopes to eventually work with mothers and educate them so they won't allow their sons to be killed by racism and oppression.

Because Delia inhabits a border crossing, she doesn't have conventional guidance from her real mother that can help her negotiate this realm. Thus she must look to surrogate mothers like her friend and teacher, Mattie, and her Aunt Marta. Delia can write her story with the help of Aunt Marta, who tells her the stories about their familial and personal history; with the help of teachers like Mattie, who provide access to Chicano history and to authors like James Joyce and Virginia Woolf; and with the help of the Chicano student movement. As have her literary foremothers, St. Teresa, Sor Juana, Delmira Agustini and others, Delia struggles with silence and censorship, both external and internal.

The worst enemy of the Chicana, sometimes, is herself for having internalized these polarities. She must call on personal conviction, support from friends, and have some basis of political awareness in order to act on her own needs. . . . By implication, a female's independent behavior is viewed as synonymous with sexual libertarianism and as being more masculine than feminine. (Garcia-Bahne 1977: 41)

At the Day of the Dead party, the liminal space is a crossroad, inhabited by guests representing real historical and literary figures from European, Anglo-American, Mexican and Mexican American cultures that represent the plurality and multivocality of Delia's mestiza consciousness. Of the characters at the Day of the Dead party, James Joyce, the original writer who challenged British and Roman Catholic authority by writing about the psychology of colonization, and St. Teresa, a female mystic who challenged church authority with her personal experiences of divinity, are the most significant. Joyce experimented with language and punctuation as did Corpi with Delia's unpunctuated interior monologues. James Joyce's novels question the dominant conception of language as well as the dominant culture's boundary of gender opposition because the "linguistic ideology that those rigid boundaries serve is continuous with the gender ideology that gives us over and over again, two sexes in fixed and unproductive opposition" (Attridge 1989: 562).

The other "dead guests" at the party represent the voices of men and women writers and rebels that signify a hidden history of literary and revolutionary ancestors. Virginia Woolf, George Sand and Emily Dickinson were women with unique life styles and literary voices. Latin American women like Delmira Agustini and Sor Juana also challenged the values of their time and culture and were controversial women writers. Before being silenced by the Bishop of Puebla, Sor Juana "exalted the rights of women, and defended slaves and South American Indians in her texts" (Buck 1992: 685). Murieta was a California rebel and outlaw, and Pancho Villa and Zapata were leaders of the Mexican peasant revolution for agrarian reform. Baudelaire, Poe, Pound and T. S. Eliot were unconventional male literary voices, and José Montoya, Luis Valdez and Alurista were authors in the Chicano literary movement. Alurista has been regarded as a significant figure in the 1965–1969 Chicano movement through his "experiments with bilingualism and the incorporation of indigenous themes in his work, and his key role as philosopher and ideologist in the . . . nationalist phase of the Movement" (Tatum 1982: 143). Luis Valdez "founded El Teatro Campesino to support the Cesar Chavez-led strike against the grape growers" and he has continued efforts on behalf of farm workers (Tatum 50). Significantly, Teatro Campesino used masks to enact the relationship between the campesino and El Patrón. Giving the campesino an opportunity to assume the role of patron and vice versa suggests the arbitrary and therefore reversible nature of these roles. "Masks become ritualized events in which the audience must participate. They invite the community to reflect upon and understand its destiny and to create a new future" (Fabre 1986: 93).

These authors at the Day of the Dead party represent an alternative to the language of academic discourse required in Delia's dissertation, which alienated her from the Spanish language of her Mexican American heritage as well as from the expressive language of political activism, poetic discourse and oral tradition. Delia's nightmares provide her with a poetic language and her Aunt Marta provides her with oral traditions that inspire her to write an autobiographical novel. In Foucault's "Dreams, Imagination and Existence," mentioned in *Cactus Blood*, he concludes that dreams are existential opportunities to liberate oneself into radical freedom. "The dream is the bearer of the deepest human meanings" (Foucault 1993: 53). After a life of satisfying others' expectations, Delia is able to spontaneously express her sexuality and translate her fantasies of Joyce into an affair with writing passionately. "The text is always written under the sweet pressure of love" (Cixous 1991: 43). Like St. Teresa, Sor Juana and Delmira, Delia's

writing has become her lover. "It was the writing that had become important. She alone lived in that world, had control over it, created chaos or order as she pleased, at times" (Corpi 1989: 108).

Delia resolves her confusion about James Joyce/Roger by finally meeting
him again near the novel's last scene. Until then she has wondered about
his recurrence in her thoughts and whether this is an obstacle to her relationship with Jeff. In this meeting, Roger explains that she was preoccupied
with him "[b]ecause you needed something to look forward to, something
that would ease the pain inside, make you forget what you had lost" (Corpi
186). During this meeting, Delia realizes that she can at last admit her love
for Jeff. In order to express her passion about love and life, Delia must re-
move the masks that have been imposed on Chicanos and the masks that silence women. She is able to do this through the stories—stories of her
family, of her culture, of historical and contemporary struggles of Chicanos
and literary stories by men and women who have refused to be silenced.
Delia resolves her state of emotional crisis through cathartic writing that
enables her to construct an authentic identity by a "certain Chicano gift for
improvisation and recombination within an array of disparate cultural elements that has been called 'transculturation' " (Rosaldo 1993: 215).

Given her historical and cultural circumstances, Delia cannot abandon
her Chicana identity or her commitment to resist and change oppression,
but she also refuses to deny herself love and the eroticism of writing.
"Woman's writing becomes 'organic writing,' 'nurturing-writing'
(nourricriture), resisting separation. It becomes a 'connoting material,' a
'kneading dough,' a 'linguistic flesh.' " (Trinh 1989: 38). Delia wants to
love passionately but also to be passionate about her life, especially her
writing. She has united the sexual ecstasy of Joyce's Molly with the mystical
ecstasy of St. Teresa and the intellectual passion of Sor Juana. Delia's ancestors include Mexican revolutionaries, European, Latin American and
Spanish authors, especially women, all of whom are relevant to her multi-
faceted identity as a working-class Mexican-American woman poet and
scholar. By overcoming her fears and writing her story of political activism,
passion and sexuality, Delia is carrying on the tradition of Asuncion her
great-grandmother, the "storyteller, the weaver of words" (Corpi 1989:
181).

NOTES

1. This idea that Delia is mourning her lost childhood was suggested to me by
Chuck Tatum, dean of humanities at the University of Arizona, and has provided
an important key to unlocking all four novels.

2. See Stephanie Merrim, *Feminist Perspectives on Sor Juana Ines de la Cruz* and Alison Weber, *Teresa of Avila and the Rhetoric of Femininity.*

6
～ Conclusion ～

The women characters in all four novels are separated from their mothers either through death or through estrangement and, in the case of Fleur and Gráinne, are also separated or alienated from their children. This relates to the split between the maternal, corporeal relationship and the paternal symbolic order. Since the body, especially the maternal body, represents the social body in miniature, the issues of social order and purity are enacted through women's bodies. "Maternal authority is the trustee of that mapping of the self's clean and proper body; it is distinguished from paternal laws" (Kristeva 1982: 72). Gráinne's mother is dead from cancer and she feels that the women in her family who died of cancer developed it as a result of their repressed rage. Ella's mother decides to entrust her to the care of Maydene so that Ella, as a racially mixed person, can experience a world beyond the Grove Town world of her mother. Fleur sends her daughter Lulu to the boarding school, perhaps because after her infant dies she feels unable to protect her remaining child from the dangers of being Anishinaabeg in an increasingly white world. Delia feels that her mother has rejected her because she is female and can't replace her dead brothers.

These characters' separations or estrangements from their mothers and children signifies the disruption of women's role in cultural reproduction which, combined with colonialism's disruption of a precolonial culture, results in a fragmented, hybrid context in which it is difficult to recover the untold, painful stories of slavery, rape and conquest and to retrieve the precolonial and maybe even prepatriarchal residual culture. The prehistoric significance of the Irish hag of sovereignty, this old-young Cailleach who rules over the threshold time of *Samhain*, when the year is renewed, has been lost. She was certainly a once powerful and awesome representative of divine power who has been reduced to an ugly hag and finally erased altogether by Catholicism until she appears as the abandoned nun, Judith, in *No Country for Young Men*. In the legendary story of Gráinne, she was a woman who could put a geis (magical injunction) on a man and force him to run away with her. In *No Country for Young Men*, Gráinne as the central character is also the young aspect of the Cailleach, who seems caught in a transgenerational repetition of the legendary love story. What does la Llorona really signify? In Mexican and Mexican-American folklore, one explanation of her weeping is that she has killed her children because of her husband's betrayal and now wanders endlessly looking for those she has lost. In Gloria Anzaldúa's reinterpretation, she is weeping over the conquest and her lost children are los Chicanos.

In all of these novels, the traditional culture and the colonized's version of history have been repressed and the repressed eventually returns often in a destructive manner, like the murders in *No Country for Young Men* or the hurricane generated by Ella's healing in *Myal*. For Delia the repressed comes through her dreams and eventually is expressed in her writing. In *Tracks*, the repressed returns through the self-destructive behavior of Pauline and through Fleur's "water monster." This breakdown of boundaries that permits the repressed to return is essential to social change and renewal. By acknowledging that paradox, these novels directly or indirectly contest the symbolic order and allude to fragments of alternative symbolic orders being re-membered by survivors.

By using processes of descent into the zone of the repressed as rites of passage, the women characters in these novels of Brodber, Corpi, O'Faolain and Erdrich rebirth themselves, forging alternative personal and historical identities as women rather than reproducing patriarchal ideologies. The narrative process of reconstructing a postcolonial identity is *unheimlich* because once the fragments resulting from colonization are reassembled there will always be gaps of unrecoverable history. By disrupting our conventional constructions of meaning, these texts create a liminal space, an "elsewhere," in which there is no rigid boundary between *eros* and *thanatos* or *heimlich* and *unheimlich*; in which madness and mysticism can constitute alternative epistemologies; and in which revised histories result from re-membering the fragmented stories. Ella, Judith and Delia all express themselves through this type of fragmentary narrative. The "Great Master" anthropologist fears these gaps or silences because they challenge his ability to create a master narrative as a method of establishing his power over the natives, just as the psychoanalyst tries to weave a cohesive narrative out of his patients' fragments, "filling in the fissures that reveal the emptiness of knowledge" (Trinh 1989: 68). The space of hybridity or borderlands that results from the cultural contact of colonialism will have fissures like the *herida abierta*, or open wound, of Anzaldúa. These authors transform fragmentation, loss and madness from negative effects of colonialism to opportunities for constructing fluid alternatives. When the symbolic order breaks down, new narrative genealogies can be created rather than a discourse of mastery.

During Nanapush's narrative, he tells a story about how Lulu froze her feet during the Skeleton Winter. This tale perhaps most movingly summarizes the regenerative power of storytelling, a pervasive motif in all the novels. Nanapush explains that he often wondered what it was like to be a woman and be able to "invent a human from the extra materials of her own body" (Erdrich 1989: 167). When he is holding and warming Lulu's feet all through the night, Nanapush has the opportunity to "give birth" because he sustains Lulu's life through his storytelling.

I talked on and on until you lost yourself inside the flow of it, until you entered the swell and ebb and did not sink but were sustained. I talked beyond sense—by morning the sounds I made were stupid mumbles without meaning or connection. But you were lulled by the roll of my voice. (Erdrich 167)

How might postcolonial women participate in this reclaiming of stories? Abena Busia reminds us that Caliban's mother, Sycorax, is silent in *The Tempest* as well as in JanMohamed's critique of colonialism: "For both colonized men and women, the texts are read collectively as an articulation of mastery, yet for the women, the articulation of that mastery is multiply problematic, resting as it does upon the silenced body of the native female" (Busia 1990: 94). Refuting Gayatri Spivak's assertion that the subaltern can't speak, Busia claims that the colonial woman is a "speaking historical subject," not voiceless and storyless as posited by colonial discourse. "In unmasking the dispossessions of the silences of fiction and the fictions of silence, we (re)construct self-understanding. Furthermore, for women, 'narrative' is not always and only, or even necessarily, a speech act" (Busia 104).

Trinh Minh-ha asserts that the memories of women were the "worlds earliest archives" (Trinh 1989: 121). Thus recovering the memories of women and their stories as an alternative to the dominant colonial discourse is essential for the female characters in these novels. However, the codification of history as a discipline has resulted in the discrediting of stories and oral traditions. By setting the factual in opposition to the fictional, "story-writing becomes history writing and history quickly sets itself apart consigning story to the realm of tale, legend, myth, fiction, literature" (Trinh 120). The female characters in all these novels speak, though their voices may be outside the dominant discourse and therefore they might be considered voiceless. Silence, which is a mark of absence viewed from a patriarchal Eurocentric perspective, could be viewed as a presence or a text from an alternative reading. "Silence is the space in narration where culture and feminine consciousness do sometimes reveal themselves, if only we can learn to decipher the psychological and cultural meanings" (Laurence 1994: 166).

All of the characters "speak" with their bodies: Fleur and Gráinne with their sexuality; Ella through the storm generated by her healing; and Delia through her masquerade as Teresa of Avila. Pauline's narrative is distorted by her internalized colonialism. Fleur's apparent silence suggests a refusal to speak the colonizer's dominant language and discourse, though she speaks with her actions. Through her colonial education, Ella, in *Myal*, has been indoctrinated by texts alien to Jamaica. As she begins to reconnect with the repressed oral texts of her culture, Ella speaks a riddle that suggests a potentially subversive discourse of resistance is emerging. Judith, in *No Country for Young Men*, is partially silenced by shock treatments and forced incarceration in a convent. When she tries to communicate what has been distorted by this violent repression, she is misunderstood. Gráinne has learned the discourse of patriarchal Catholicism and nationalism, though she is resisting this discourse in a fragmentary way while attempting to understand Judith's fragmented speech. Delia has used the dominant discourse to acquire her Ph.D. but ultimately finds a poetic literary voice more appropriate to express the disruptive fragments surfacing through dreams and interior monologue.

Women of colonized cultures must resist the silencing by language loss as well as by dominant ideologies that exclude subaltern voices from discourse. Carole Boyce Davies explains the apparent voicelessness of Caribbean women in a manner that might apply to the female characters in all four postcolonial novels. Voicelessness can mean the absence of women's written texts, but it can also mean the inability or unwillingness of women to express themselves in the master's language and thus the likelihood of being unheard (Davies and Fido 1990: 1). Ella evolves from a state of voiceless zombification to a woman capable of participating in collective resistance to colonialism by recovering knowledge of the "half that hasn't been told," a recurring phrase in *Myal*. In *No Country for Young Men*, Judith is partially able to recover the repressed story of Sparky's death and Gráinne is able to recover the eroticism repressed by Irish Catholicism. At the end of *Tracks*, Fleur disappears, using invisibility as a resistance strategy only after she has first enacted the disappearance of the forest coveted by the lumber companies. She is a trickster hidden on the margins of the novel, half-bear and half-woman, whose story is being passed on through Pauline's and Nanapush's oral traditions. Delia begins her recovery from *susto* at the Day of the Dead party when her masquerade as St. Teresa permits her to shed the socially imposed masks. She is finally able to express her voice through storytelling genealogies that include both oral and print traditions. Cultural reproduction and narrative genealogies, or who transmits stories to whom and how, is a significant component of familial and cultural continuity and resistance to colonialism in the four texts. Although stories are stolen or distorted by the colonizer, the decolonized subject is born by recovering these erased or repressed stories of survival.

The remembering of these oral stories is essential to the recovery process of the women in these novels. The women characters validate oral storytelling as an expression of the repressed oral tradition that resurfaces through Ella's riddle, Aunt Marta's ancestral stories, Judith's story of the fairy otherworld and the folklore and narratives of Fleur's life as told by Nanapush and Pauline. "Storytelling [is] the oldest form of building historical consciousness" and sustaining a living tradition (Trinh 1989: 148). These four authors—Erdrich, Brodber, O'Faolain and Corpi—recover personal and cultural histories and weave a web of narrative kinship through storytelling, both their own and that of their female characters. While the characters in each novel are situated in a unique sociocultural context defined by different colonial influences, different precolonial traditions and different forms of sexual repression, they all express the conflicts and ambiguities of existing in a borderland and construct stories that challenge the master discourse of colonialism or create female narrative genealogies. As stated by De Lauretis, "The conceptual and discursive space of a female genealogy can effectively mediate a woman's relation to the symbolic, allowing her self-definition as female being, or female-gendered speaking subject" (De Lauretis 1989: 15). This woman-centered identity must be founded on the woman's specific historical and cultural location as well as on her intellectual relation to a network of women's stories.

Tell me and let me tell my hearers what I have heard from you who heard it from your mother and your grandmother, so that what is said may be guarded and unfailingly transmitted to the women of tomorrow, who will be our children and the children of our children. (Trinh 1989: 122)

These women authors reclaim women's role in cultural reproduction through the transmittal of stories that empower women by allowing them to inhabit their bodies and their history, however painful. Thus women can construct narrative kinship by passing on stories which express the relationship of the personal and the political through the lens of female subjectivity.

While the novels' characters exist in a culturally liminal space mingling precolonial and postcolonial elements as well as blurring boundaries between life and death, madness and sanity, each of the novels contains a space or time that acts as a creative liminal zone from which the repressed returns as well as fertile ground from which alternative stories emerge. In *Tracks*, the area around Matchimanito Lake represents this zone: "The water there was surrounded by the highest oaks, by woods inhabited by ghosts and roamed by Pillagers" and the supernatural Misshepeshu resides in the lake. (Erdrich 1989: 2). The bog, which constitutes this liminal zone in *No Country for Young Men*, is associated with historical memory, the fairy mounds of prehistoric Ireland, the mental confusion of Judith and the erotic adventure of Gráinne. In *Myal*, the year 1919 is a liminal time when a strike wave in Jamaica led to the legalization of unions and when events around the world, such as the declaration of Irish independence and strikes throughout the United States, heralded a potential for change that is signified by Ella's ability to generate a cathartic storm. The Day of the Dead party in *Delia's Song* is a liminal event occurring at a threshold time in a milieu with dead literary and historical figures, whose stories made Delia's life as a college-educated Chicana possible, just as her life story could create possibilities for subsequent generations.

All of these texts are haunted by the past, by memories of the dead and the social and historical traumas that caused their deaths. Ruptures of the fragmented, repressed history erupt into the texts, creating a dialogue between official history and the unspeakable story of oppression and loss. History is always ambiguous and this allows once acceptable interpretations to be countered by alternative interpretations, constructed as much by the emotion and imagination of oral tradition and dreams as by "facts."

∾ References ∾

Acuña, Rodolfo. *Occupied America: The Chicanos Struggle toward Liberation*. San Francisco: Canfield, 1972.

Alarcón, Norma. "Traddutora, Traditora: A Paradigmatic Figure of Chicana Feminism." *Cultural Critique* (Fall 1989): 57–87.

Alexander, M. Jacqui and Mohanty, Chandra Talpade. *Feminist Genealogies, Colonial Legacies, Democratic Futures*. New York: Routledge, 1997.

Anzaldúa, Gloria. *Borderlands-La Frontera*. San Francisco: Spinsters/Aunt Lute, 1987.

———. *Making Face, Making Soul: Haciendo Caras*. San Francisco: Aunt Lute, 1990.

Arata, Stephen D. "The Occidental Tourist: *Dracula* and the Anxiety of Reverse Colonization." *Victorian Studies* 33:4 (1990): 621–45.

Arensberg, Conrad. *The Irish Countryman*. Garden City, N.Y.: Natural History Press, 1968.

Attridge, Derek. "Molly's Flow: The Writing of Penelope and the Question of Women's Language." *Modern Fiction Studies* 35:3 (1989): 543–65.

Babcock, Barbara. "At Home, No Womens Are Storytellers: Potteries, Stories and Politics in Cochiti Pueblo." *Journal of the Southwest* 30:3 (1988): 356–89.

Babcock-Abrahams, Barbara. " 'A Tolerated Margin of Mess': The Trickster and His Tales Reconsidered." *Journal of Folklore Institute* 11:3 (1975): 147–86.

Barnouw, Victor. *Wisconsin Chippewa Myths*. Madison: University of Wisconsin, 1977.

Barrett, Leonard. *The Rastafarians: Sounds of Cultural Dissonance*. Boston: Beacon, 1994.

Benjamin, Jessica. *Bonds of Love: Psychoanalysis, Feminism, and the Problem of Domination*. New York: Pantheon, 1988.

Bergner, Gwen. "Who Is That Masked Woman: Or, the Role of Gender in Fanon's *Black Skin, White Masks.*" *PMLA* 110:1 (1995): 75–88.

Bhaba, Homi. "Signs Taken for Wonders: Questions of Ambivalence and Authority under a Tree Outside Delhi, May 1817." *Critical Inquiry* 12 (Autumn 1985): 144–65.

Bird, Gloria. "Searching for Evidence of Colonialism at Work: A Reading of Louise Erdrich's *Tracks.*" *Wicazo Review* 8:2 (1992): 40–47.

Boland, Eavan. *A Kind of Scar: The Woman Poet in a National Tradition.* Dublin: Attic, 1989.

———. "Mise Éire." *Outside History: Selected Poems, 1980–1990.* New York: W. W. Norton, 1990.

Bourgeois, Arthur, ed. *Ojibwa Narratives of Charles Kawbawgam and Jacques Le Pique 1893–95.* Detroit: Wayne State, 1994.

Bourke, Angela. "Language, Stories, Healing" in *Gender and Sexuality in Modern Ireland,* ed. Anthony Bradley and Maryann Gialanella Valiulis. Amherst: University of Massachusetts, 1997.

———. "Reading a Woman's Death: Colonial Text and Oral Tradition in Nineteenth-Century Ireland." *Feminist Studies* 21:3 (1995): 553–86.

———. "The Virtual Reality of Irish Fairy Legend." *Eire-Ireland* 31:1–2 (1996): 7–25.

Bradley, Anthony and Gialanella Valiulis, Maryann, eds. *Gender and Sexuality in Modern Ireland.* Amherst: University of Massachusetts, 1997.

Brady, Ciaran. "Constructive and Instrumental: The Dilemma of Ireland's First 'New Historians' " in *Interpreting Irish History: The Debate on Historical Revisionism 1938–1994,* ed. Ciaran Brady. Dublin: Irish Academic Press, 1994.

Braidotti, Rosi. *Patterns of Dissonance,* trans. Elizabeth Guild. New York: Routledge, 1991.

Brathwaite, Edward Kamau. "Caliban, Ariel, and Unprospero in the Conflict of Creolization: A Study of the Slave Revolt in Jamaica, 1831–32." *Annals of the New York Academy of Sciences* 292 (1977): 41–62.

———. *Development of Creole Society in Jamaica 1770–1820.* Oxford: Oxford University, 1971.

Brehm, Victoria. "The Metamorphoses of an Ojibwa Manido." *American Literature* 68:4 (1996): 677–706.

Brodber, Erna. "Fiction in the Scientific Procedure" in *Caribbean Women Writers: Essays from the First International Conference,* ed. Selwyn Cudjoe. Amherst: University of Massachusetts, 1990. 164–68.

———. *Jane and Louisa Will Soon Come Home.* London: New Beacon, 1980.

———. *Louisiana.* Jackson: University Press of Mississippi, 1994.

———. *Myal.* London: New Beacon, 1988.

———. "Oral Sources and the Creation of the Social History of the Caribbean." *Jamaica Journal* 16:4 (1983): 2–10.

Brodber, Erna and Green, J. E. *Reggae and Cultural Identity in Jamaica: Working Papers on Caribbean Society.* St. Augustine, Trinidad: University of West Indies, 1981.

Brogan, Kathleen. "Haunted by History: Louise Erdrich's *Tracks.*" *Prospects* 21 (1996): 169–92.

Brontë, Charlotte. *Jane Eyre.* New York: W. W. Norton, 1971.

Buck, Claire. *The Bloomsbury Guide to Women's Literature.* New York: Prentice-Hall, 1992.

Busia, Abena. "Silencing Sycorax: On African Colonial Discourse and the Unvoiced Female." *Cultural Critique* (winter 1990): 81–104.

Canny, Nicholas P. *The Elizabethan Conquest of Ireland: A Pattern Established 1565–76.* New York: Barnes and Noble, 1976.

———. "The Ideology of English Colonization: From Ireland to America." *William and Mary Quarterly* 3rd ser., vol. 30 (1973): 575–98.

Carlyle, Thomas. "The Nigger Question." *Critical and Miscellaneous Essays Vol. VII.* London: Chapman and Hall, 1872. 79–110.

Carmichael, Elizabeth. *The Skeleton at the Feast.* Austin: University of Texas, 1992.

Césaire, Aimé. *Discourse on Colonialism.* New York: Monthly Review Press, 1972.

———. *Une Tempête.* trans. by Richard Miller. New York: Ubu Repertory, 1985.

Chevannes, Barry. *Rastafari and Other African-Caribbean Worldviews.* The Hague: Macmillan, in association with the Institute of Social Sciences, 1998.

———. *Rastafari: Roots and Ideology.* Syracuse: Syracuse University, 1994.

Cixous, Hélène. *Coming to Writing.* Cambridge: Harvard University Press, 1991.

———. "The Laugh of the Medusa" in *New French Feminisms,* ed. Elaine Marks and Isabelle de Coutivron. New York: Schocken, 1980. 245–64.

Clarke, Joni. "Why Bears Are Good to Think and Theory Doesn't Have to be Murder: Transformation and Oral Tradition in Louise Erdrich's *Tracks.*" *Study of American Indian Literatures* 4:1(1992): 28–48.

Cooper, Carolyn. "Afro-Jamaican Folk Elements in Brodber's *Jane and Louisa Will Soon Come Home*" in *Out of the Kumbla: Caribbean Women and Literature,* ed. Carole Boyce Davies and Elaine Savory Fido. Trenton, N.J.: Africa World Press, 1990.

———. *Noises in the Blood: Orality, Gender and the "Vulgar" Body of Jamaican Popular Culture.* Durham, N.C.: Duke University, 1993.

Corbin, Alain. "Commercial Sexuality in Nineteenth-Century France." *Representations* 14 (1986): 209–19.

Corpi, Lucha. *Cactus Blood.* Houston: Arte Público, University of Houston, 1995.

———. *Delia's Song.* Houston: Arte Público, University of Houston, 1989.

———. *Eulogy for a Brown Angel.* Houston: Arte Público, University of Houston, 1992.

Costigan, Giovanni. *History of Modern Ireland.* New York: Pegasus, 1970.

Cotelli, Laura. *Winged Words: American Indian Writers Speak.* Lincoln: University of Nebraska, 1990.

Curtis, Edmund. *A History of Ireland.* (1936 reprint) London: Methuen, 1970.

Curtis, L. Perry, Jr. *Apes and Angels: The Irishman in Victorian Caricature.* Washington D.C.: Smithsonian, 1971.

Cypess, Sandra Messinger. *La Malinche in Mexican Literature.* Austin: University of Texas, 1991.

Danziger, Edward Jefferson, Jr. *The Chippewas of Lake Superior.* Norman: University of Oklahoma, 1977.

Davies, Carole Boyce and Fido, Elaine Savory, eds. *Out of the Kumbla: Caribbean Women and Literature.* Trenton, New Jersey: Africa World Press, 1990.

Dayan, Joan. "Playing Caliban: Césaire's Tempest." *Arizona Quarterly* 48:4 (1992): 125–45.

Deane, Seamus. "Joyce the Irishman" in *The Cambridge Companion to James Joyce,* ed. Derek Attridge. New York: Cambridge University Press, 1990. 31–53.

De Lauretis, Teresa. "The Essence of the Triangle or, Taking the Risk of Essentialism Seriously: Feminist Theory in Italy, the U.S. and Britain." *Differences* 1:2 (1989): 1–37.

———. *Feminist Studies/Critical Studies.* Bloomington: Indiana University Press, 1986.

Dijkstra, Bram. *Idols of Perversity.* New York: Oxford University Press, 1986.

Donnelly, James. "The Construction of the Memory of the Famine in Ireland and the Irish Diaspora, 1850–1900. *Eire/Ireland* 31:1–2 (1996): 26–61.

Douglas, Mary. *Purity and Danger.* New York: Ark, 1989.

Duffy, Maureen. *The Erotic World of Faery.* London: Hodder and Stoughton, 1972.

Duran, Eduardo and Duran, Bonnie. *Native American Postcolonial Psychology.* Albany: State University of New York, 1995.

Eagleton, Terry. *Heathcliff and the Great Hunger: Studies in Irish Culture.* New York: Verso, 1995.

Eagleton, Terry, Frederic Jameson, and Edward W. Said. *Nationalism, Colonialism and Literature.* Minneapolis: University of Minnesota Press, 1990.

Encyclopaedia Britannica, 15th ed. "Marcus Garvey" Chicago: Encyclopaedia Britannica, 1995.

Erdrich, Louise. *The Bingo Palace.* New York: Harper, 1995.

———. *Jacklight.* New York: Henry Holt, 1984.

———. *Tracks.* New York: Harper and Row, 1989.

Fabre, Genevieve. "Dialectics of the Masks in El Teatro Campesino: From Images to Ritualized Events" in *Missions in Conflict: Essays on U.S.-Mexican Relations and Chicano Culture,* ed. Renate von Bardeleben. Tubingen: G. Narr, 1986. 93–99.

Fanon, Frantz. *Black Skin, White Masks,* trans. Charles Markmann. New York: Grove, 1982.

Foucault, Michel. "Dreams, Imagination and Existence" in *Dream and Existence,* ed. Keith Hoeller. Atlantic Highlands, N.J.: Humanities Press, 1993

Fox-Lockert, Lucia. "Amorous Fantasies." *Americas* 39:1 (1987): 38–41.

Freud, Sigmund. "The Uncanny." *Standard Edition of the Complete Psychological Works of Sigmund Freud*, vol. 17, ed. James Strachey and Anna Freud. London: Hogarth, 1919. 368–407.

Galindo, D. Letticia and Gonzales, Maria Dolores. *Speaking Chicana: Voice, Power and Identity.* Tucson: University of Arizona, 1999.

Garcia, Ignacio. *The Rise and Fall of La Raza Unida Party.* Tucson: University of Arizona, 1989.

Garcia-Bahne, Betty. "La Chicana and the Chicano Family" in *Essays on La Mujer*, ed. Rosaura Sanchez and Rosa Martinez Cruz. Los Angeles: Univesity of California, 1977. 34–47.

Geertz, Clifford. *The Interpretation of Cultures.* New York: Basic, 1973.

Hallowell, A. Irving. "Ojibwa Ontology, Behavior, and World View" in *Teachings from the American Earth*, ed. Dennis Tedlock and Barbara Tedlock. New York: Liveright, 1975. 141–77.

Hanks, Patrick and Hodges, Flavia. *A Dictionary of Surnames.* New York: Oxford University Press, 1988.

Harjo, Joy and Bird, Gloria. *Reinventing the Enemy's Language: Contemporary Native Women's Writing.* New York: Norton, 1997.

Harvey, Clodagh Brennan. "Some Irish Women Storytellers and Reflections on the Role of Women in the Storytelling Tradition." *Western Folklore* 48 (1989): 109–28.

Heaney, Seamus. *Preoccupations: Selected Prose 1968–1978.* New York: Farrar, Straus, Giroux, 1980.

Heilbrun, Carolyn. *Writing a Woman's Life.* New York: Ballantine, 1988.

Herr, Cheryl. "The Erotics of Irishness." *Critical Inquiry* 17 (1990): 1–34.

Herrmann, Claudine. *The Tongue Snatchers*, trans. Nancy Kline. Lincoln: University of Nebraska, 1989.

Hirsch, Edward. "The Imaginary Irish Peasant." *PMLA* 106:5 (1991): 1116–33.

Hulme, Peter. *Colonial Encounters.* London: Methuen, 1986.

Hunter, Dianne. "Hysteria, Psychoanalysis and Feminism: The Case of Anna O." *Feminist Studies* 9:3 (1983): 465–89.

Hurston, Zora Neale. *Tell My Horse.* New York: Harper & Row, 1990.

Irigaray, Luce. *This Sex Which Is Not One*, trans. by Catherine Porter. Ithaca: Cornell University Press, 1985.

Jaggar, Alison M. "Love and Knowledge: Emotion in Feminist Epistemology" in *Gender/Body/Knowledge: Feminist Reconstructions of Being and Knowing*, ed. Alison Jaggar and Susan Bordo. New Brunswick, N.J.: Rutgers University, 1989. 145–71.

JanMohamed, Abdul. "The Economy of Manichean Allegory: The Function of Racial Difference in Colonialist Literature" in *"Race," Writing and Difference*, ed. Henry Louis Gates. Chicago: University of Chicago, 1986. 78–106.

———. *Manichean Aesthetics.* Amherst: University of Massachusetts, 1983.

Joyce, James. *Portrait of the Artist as a Young Man.* New York: Penguin, 1977.

Kahane, Claire. "Why Dora Now?" in *In Dora's Case: Freud-Hysteria-Feminism*, ed. Charles Bernheimer and Claire Kahane. New York: Columbia University Press, 1985. 19–32.

Kamboureli, Smaro. "St. Teresa's Jouissance: Towards a Rhetoric of Reading the Sacred" in *Silence, the Word and the Sacred*, ed. E. D. Blodgett and H. G. Coward. Calgary: Wilfrid Laurier University, 1989. 51–63.

Kaplan, Irving, Howard Blutstein, Kathryn Therese Johnston, and David McMorris. *Area Handbook for Jamaica*. Washington, D.C.: U.S. Government Printing Office, 1976.

Kearney, Richard. *Myth and Motherland*. Field Day Pamphlet 5. Derry: Field Day Theatre Company, 1984.

Kearney, Richard, ed. *Across the Frontiers: Ireland in the 1990s*. Dublin: Wolfhound Press, 1988.

Killian, D. "Worth Celebrating: The Women's Liberation Movement in Ireland." *Sojourner* 21:11 (1996): 7–8.

Knuth, Elizabeth. "The Gift of Tears in Teresa of Avila." *Mystics Quarterly* 20:4 (1994): 131–42.

Kramb, Marie. "Review of *Teresa of Avila and the Rhetoric of Femininity*." *Religion and Literature* 24:3 (1992): 111–12.

Kristeva, Julia. *The Powers of Horror: An Essay on Abjection*. New York: Columbia, 1982.

Krystal, Henry. "Integration and Self-Healing in Post-Traumatic States." *American Imago* 48:1 (1991): 93–118.

Landes, Ruth. *Ojibwa Religion and the Midéwiwin*. Madison: University of Wisconsin, 1986.

Laurence, Patricia. "Women's Silence as a Ritual of Truth: A Study of Literary Expressions in Austen, Brontë and Woolf" in *Listening to Silences: New Essays in Feminist Criticism*, ed. Elaine Hedges and Shelly Fisher Fishkin. New York: Oxford University Press, 1994.

Lewis, Matthew Gregory. *Journal of a Residence among the Negroes in the West Indies*. London: J. Murray, 1845.

Lincoln, Kenneth. *Native American Renaissance*. Berkeley: University of California, 1985.

Litton, Helen. *The Irish Famine: an Illustrated History*. Dublin: Wolfhound, 1994.

Lopez Springfield, Consuelo, ed. *Daughters of Caliban: Caribbean Women in the Twentieth Century*. Bloomington: Indiana University Press, 1997.

Mac Cana, Proinsias. "Sídh" in *Encyclopedia of Religion*, ed. Mircea Eliade. New York: Macmillan, 1987.

Maddox, Brenda. *Nora: The Real Life of Molly Bloom*. Boston: Houghton Mifflin, 1988.

Markale, Jean. *Women of the Celts*, trans. A. Mygind and C. Hauch. Rochester, Vt.: Inner Traditions, 1986.

Mazzoni, Cristina. "Feminism, Abjection, Transgression: Angela of Foligno and the Twentieth Century." *Mystics Quarterly* 17:2 (1991): 61–70.

McClintock, Anne. "The Angel of Progress: Pitfalls of the Term Post-Colonialism." *Social Text* 31/32 (1992): 84–98.

———. "The Very House of Difference: Race, Gender, and the Politics of South African Women's Narrative in *Poppie Nongena*" in *The Bounds of Race*. ed. Dominick La Capra. Ithaca: Cornell University Press, 1991. 196–230.

Merrim, Stephanie. "Toward a Feminist Reading of Sor Juana Inés de la Cruz: Past, Present, and Future Directions in Sor Juana Criticism" in *Feminist Perspectives on Sor Juana Inés de la Cruz*, ed. Stephanie Merrim. Detroit: Wayne State, 1991. 11–37.

Moquin, Wayne, ed. *A Documentary History of the Mexican Americans*. New York: Bantam, 1972.

Moraga, Cherríe. *Loving in the War Years: Lo Que Nunca Pasó por Sus Labios*. Boston: South End, 1983.

Moraga, Cherríe and Anzaldúa, Gloria, eds. *This Bridge Called My Back: Writings by Radical Women of Color*. New York: Kitchen Table/Women of Color Press, 1983.

Morales, Rosario and Levins Morales, Aurora. *Getting Home Alive*. Ithaca: Firebrand, 1986.

Morrison, Toni. *Beloved*. New York: Knopf, 1987.

———. "Unspeakable Things Unspoken: The Afro-American Presence in American Literature." *Michigan Quarterly Review* 18:1 (1989): 1–34.

Mullin, Molly. "Representations of History, Irish Feminism, and the Politics of Difference." *Feminist Studies* 17:1 (1991): 29–50.

Muñoz, Jr., Carlos. *Youth, Identity, Power: The Chicano Movement*. New York: Verso, 1989.

Norat, Gisela. "Vampirismo, Sadismo y Masoquismo en la Poesia de Delmira Agustini." *Linguistica y Literatura* 17 (1990): 152–64.

O'Callaghan, Evelyn. "The Bottomless Abyss: 'Mad' Women in Some Caribbean Novels." *Bulletin of East Caribbean Affairs* 11:1 (1985): 45–58.

O'Connor, John. *The Workhouses of Ireland: The Fate of Ireland's Poor*. Dublin: Anvil Books, 1995.

O'Connor, Sinéad. "People Need a Short, Sharp Shock," *Time*, 9 Nov. 1992, 78.

O'Connor, Theresa, ed. *Comic Tradition in Irish Women Writers*. Gainesville: University Press of Florida, 1996.

O'Faolain, Julia. *No Country for Young Men*. New York: Carroll and Graf, 1980.

Ortner, Sherry B. "Is Female to Male as Nature Is to Culture?" in *Women, Culture and Society*. ed. Michelle Zimbalist Rosaldo and Louise Lamphere. Stanford: Stanford University Press, 1974. 67–87.

Otis, D. S. *The Dawes Act and the Allotment of Indian Lands*. Norman: University of Oklahoma, 1973.

Parry, Benita. "Problems in Current Theories of Colonial Discourse." *Oxford Literary Review* 9:1–2 (1987): 27–58.

Partridge, Angela. "Wild Men and Wailing Women." *Éigse* 18 (1980): 25–37.

Patterson, Orlando. *Slavery and Social Death: A Comparative Study.* Cambridge: Harvard, 1982.

Paz, Octavio. *The Labyrinth of Solitude: Life and Thought in Mexico.* New York: Grove, 1961.

Pearce, Roy Harvey. *Savagism and Civilization: A Study of the Indian and the American Mind.* Berkeley: University of California, 1988.

Perez, Emma. "Irigaray's Female Symbolic in the Making of Chicana Lesbian Sitios y Lenguas (Sites and Discourses) in *Living Chicana Theory,* ed. Carla Trujillo. Berkeley: Third Woman Press, 1998. 87–101.

Póirtéir, Cathal. *The Great Irish Famine.* Dublin: Mercier Press, 1995.

Pratt, Mary Louise. "Arts of the Contact Zone." *Profession* (1991): 33–40.

Puri, Shalini. "An 'Other' Realism: Erna Brodber's *Myal.*" *Ariel* 24:3 (1993): 96–115.

Rainwater, Catherine. "Reading Between Worlds: Narrativity in the Fiction of Louise Erdrich." *American Literature* 62:3 (1990): 405–22.

Rebolledo, Tey. *Women Singing in the Snow.* Tucson: University of Arizona, 1995.

Retamar, Roberto Fernandez. "Caliban: Notes towards a Discussion of Culture in Our America," trans. Lynn Garafola, David Arthur McMurray and Robert Marquez. *Massachusetts Review* 15 (1974): 7–72.

Rhys, Jean. *Wide Sargasso Sea.* New York: W.W. Norton, 1982.

Rosaldo, Renato. *Culture and Truth: The Remaking of Social Analysis.* Boston: Beacon, 1993.

Rosales, F. Arturo. *Chicano! The History of the Mexican American Civil Rights Movement.* Houston: Arte Publico, 1997.

Rubel, Arthur, Carl W. O'Nell and Rolando Collado-Ardón. *Susto: A Folk Illness.* Berkeley: University of California, 1984.

Saldívar, Ramon. *Chicano Narrative: The Dialectics of Difference.* Madison: University of Wisconsin, 1990.

Sánchez, Marta Ester. *Contemporary Chicana Poetry.* Berkeley: University of California, 1985.

Sayer, Chloe. *The Mexican Day of the Dead.* Boston: Shambhala, 1990.

Scheper-Hughes, Nancy. "The Best of Two Worlds, The Worst of Two Worlds: Reflections on Culture and Field Work among the Rural Irish and Pueblo Indians." *Comparative Studies in Society and History* 29:1 (1987): 56–75.

———. *Saints, Scholars and Schizophrenics: Mental Illness in Rural Ireland.* Berkeley: University of California, 1979.

Schuler, Monica. "Myalism and the African Religious Tradition in Jamaica" in *Africa and the Caribbean: Legacies of a Link,* ed. Margaret Grahan and Franklin Knight. Baltimore: Johns Hopkins University Press, 1979. 65–79.

Shakespeare, William. *The Tempest.* New York: New American Library, 1987.

Sharp, Henry. "Giant Fish, Giant Otters, and Dinosaurs 'Apparently Irrational Beliefs' in a Chipewyan Community." *American Ethnologist* 14 (1987): 226–35.

Shohat, Ella. "Notes on the Post-Colonial." *Social Text* 31/32 (1992): 99–113.

Shoshan, Tamar. "Mourning and Longing from Generation to Generation." *American Journal of Psychotherapy* 43:2 (1989): 193–207.

Showalter, Elaine. "Feminist Criticism in the Wilderness." *Critical Inquiry* 8:2 (1981): 179–205.

Sistren with Honor Ford-Smith. *Lionheart Gal: Life Stories of Jamaican Women.* London: Women's Press, 1986.

Snyder, Gary. *The Practice of the Wild.* San Francisco: North Point, 1990.

Sobo, Elisa J. "Menstrual Taboos, Witchcraft Babies and Social Relations: Women's Health Traditions in Rural Jamaica" in *Daughters of Caliban: Caribbean Women in the Twentieth Century,* ed. Consuelo Lopez Springfield. Bloomington: Indiana University Press, 1997.

Spenser, Edmund. *A View of the Present State of Ireland,* ed. W. L. Renwick. Oxford: Clarendon Press, 1970.

Spivak, Gayatri. "Can the Subaltern Speak?" in *Marxism and the Interpretation of Culture,* ed. Cary Nelson and Lawrence Grossberg. Urbana: University of Illinois, 1988. 271–313.

———. "Three Women's Texts and a Critique of Imperialism." *Critical Inquiry* 12 (1985): 243–46.

Spurr, David. "Myths of Anthropology: Eliot, Joyce, Levy-Bruhl." *PMLA* 109 (1994): 266–80.

Stallybrass, Peter and White, Allon. *The Politics and Poetics of Transgression.* Ithaca, N.Y.: Cornell, 1986.

Stanley, Sandra Kumamoto, ed. *Other Sisterhoods: Literary Theory and U.S. Women of Color.* Urbana: University of Illinois, 1998.

Tatum, Charles. *Chicano Literature.* Boston: Twayne, 1982.

Tompkins, Jane. "Me and My Shadow." *New Literary History* 19 (1987): 169–78.

Trager, James. *The People's Chronology.* New York: Henry Holt, 1992.

Trinh T. Minh-ha. *Woman, Native, Other: Postcoloniality and Feminism.* Bloomington: Indiana University Press, 1989.

Turner, Victor. *The Ritual Process.* Chicago: Aldine, 1969.

Tyler, Stephen A. "Post-Modern Ethnography: From Document of the Occult to Occult Document" in *Writing Culture: The Poetics and Politics of Ethnography,* ed. James Clifford and George E. Marcus. Berkeley: University of California, 1986. 122–40.

Vecsey, Christopher. *Traditional Ojibwa Religion and Its Historical Changes.* Philadelphia: American Philosophical Society, 1983.

Vergès, Françoise. "Creole Skin, Black Mask: Fanon and Disavowal." *Critical Inquiry* 23:3 (1997): 578–95.

Viney, Michael "Geared for a Gale," *Irish Times,* 24 Sept. 1980, 12.

Vizenor, Gerald. *The People Named the Chippewa.* Minneapolis: University of Minnesota, 1984.

Walker-Johnson, Joyce. "Myal: Text and Context." *Journal of West Indian Literature* 5:1–2 (1992): 48–64.

Waters, Anita. *Race, Class and Political Symbols: Rastafari and Reggae in Jamaican Politics*. New Brunswick, N.J.: Transaction, 1985.

Waters, John. "Confronting the Ghost of Our Past," *Irish Times*, 11 Oct. 1994, Internet, January 1996.

———. "Why the Ex-Slave Sounds Like the Oppressor," *Irish Times*, 14 March 1995, Internet, January 1996.

Weber, Alison. *Teresa of Avila and the Rhetoric of Femininity*. New York: Princeton University, 1990.

Weekes, Ann. " 'An Origin Like Water': The Poetry of Eavan Boland and Modernist Critiques of Irish Literature." in *Irishness and (Post) Modernism*, ed. John Richard. London: Bucknell University, 1994. 159–76.

———. "Diarmuid and Gráinne Again: Julia O'Faolain's *No Country for Young Men*." *Eire-Ireland* 21:1 (1986): 89–102.

———. *Irish Women Writers*. Lexington: University of Kentucky, 1990.

Wiget, Andrew. "His Life in His Tail: The Native American Trickster and the Literature of Possibility" in *Redefining American Literary History*, ed. A. La Vonne Brown Ruoff and Jerry W. Ward, Jr. New York: Modern Language Association, 1990.

———. *Native American Literature*. Boston: Twayne, 1985.

Women's Studies International Forum. Special issue "Feminism in Ireland" 11:4 (1988).

Wynter, Sylvia. "Beyond Miranda's Meanings: Un/silencing the 'Demonic Ground' of Caliban's 'Woman' " in *Out of the Kumbla*, ed. Carole Boyce Davies and Elaine Savory Fido. Trenton: Africa World Press, 1990. 355–72.

~ Index ~

About the Author

JEANNE ARMSTRONG is a librarian for the College of Arts and Sciences, Western Washington University. Dr. Armstrong holds a Ph.D. in Comparative Cultural and Literary Studies. She has served as a librarian at the Chicago Public Library and curator for the anthropology archives and manuscript collections at the Arizona State Museum, University of Arizona. Her earlier publications have appeared in *Museum Archivist Newsletter* and *Journal of the Southwest*.

Lightning Source UK Ltd.
Milton Keynes UK
19 January 2011

166022UK00005B/204/P